A Disciple's Heart

Growing in Love and Grace

Daily Workbook

James A. Harnish
with Justin LaRosa

Abingdon Press
Nashville

A DISCIPLE'S HEART:
GROWING IN LOVE AND GRACE

This book is printed on elemental, chlorine-free paper.
ISBN 978-1-63088-255-6

Scripture quotations unless noted otherwise are from the Common English Bible. Copyright © 2011 by the Common English Bible. All rights reserved. Used by permission. www.CommonEnglishBible.com.

Scripture quotations marked NRSV are from the New Revised Standard Version of the Bible, copyright 1989, Division of Christian Education of the National Council of the Churches of Christ in the United States of America. Used by permission. All rights reserved.

Scripture quotations marked KJV are from The Authorized (King James) Version. Rights in the Authorized Version in the United Kingdom are vested in the Crown. Reproduced by permission of the Crown's patentee, Cambridge University Press.

Scripture quotations marked "NKJV™" are taken from the New King James Version®. Copyright © 1982 by Thomas Nelson, Inc. Used by permission. All rights reserved.

Scripture quotations marked NIV are from the Holy Bible, New International Version®, NIV®. Copyright © 1973, 1978, 1984, 2011 by Biblica, Inc.™ Used by permission of Zondervan. All rights reserved worldwide. www.zondervan.com. The "NIV" and "New International Version" are trademarks registered in the United States Patent and Trademark Office by Biblica, Inc.™

Scripture quotations marked *The Message* are from *The Message*. Copyright © by Eugene H. Peterson 1993, 1994, 1995, 1996, 2000, 2001, 2002. Used by permission of NavPress Publishing Group.

Scripture quotations marked GNT are from the Good News Translation in Today's English Version-Second Edition © 1992 by American Bible Society. Used by Permission.

2015 2016 2017 2018 2019 2020 2021 2022 2023 2024—10 9 8 7 6 5 4 3 2 1
MANUFACTURED IN THE UNITED STATES OF AMERICA

ACKNOWLEDGMENTS

I write with immeasurable gratitude for twenty-two years of ministry with the staff and laity of Hyde Park United Methodist Church in Tampa, Florida. Like *A Disciple's Path*, this resource grew out of our life together in the mission of "making disciples of Jesus Christ for the transformation of the world." Any way the Spirit of God can use this resource in the lives of individual disciples and in other congregations will be a gift of joy for us.

I give thanks for the partnership with Justin LaRosa—who never hesitated to give ruthlessly honest feedback, wrote the "Overview of *A Disciple's Path*," created the reflection questions and guides to prayer and action in this workbook, and wrote the accompanying leader guide.

I thank my God every time I remember you, constantly praying with joy in every one of my prayers for all of you, because of your sharing in the gospel from the first day until now. I am confident of this, that the one who began a good work among you will bring it to completion by the day of Jesus Christ.

(Philippians 1:3-6 NRSV)

CONTENTS

INTRODUCTION

A Disciple's Heart continues the journey we began in our previous study, *A Disciple's Path*, by providing a framework for ongoing growth in discipleship in the Wesleyan tradition. (If you are unfamiliar with that study, read "An Overview of *A Disciple's Path*" found on pages 9–13 for a brief summary of both the framework and the spiritual disciplines by which followers of Christ are continually centering their lives in loving God and loving others.)

Our focus in this resource is the ongoing *transformation of the heart* that happens as the love of God that came among us in Jesus takes up residence in us, enabling us to become agents of God's transforming love at work in the world.

A Matter of the Heart

Have you ever felt as if you were the Tin Man in *The Wizard of Oz*? The one thing he needed was a new heart. John Wesley would affirm the gospel message and say that is true of all of us!

If we were to squeeze the central message of this study into one sentence, it would be this: "The heart of the matter is always a matter of the heart." In contrast to the Reformed tradition, which finds its starting point in right belief, the Wesleyan tradition finds its center in the transformed heart as the love of God redirects our passions, restores our relationships with God and others, and reshapes our lives into the likeness of Christ.

That is, of course, where the Wesleyan revival in England began. On the evening of May 24, 1738, a stuffy, well-educated, deeply devoted but spiritually hungry Anglican priest named John Wesley went reluctantly to a small group Bible study in Aldersgate Street in London. He wrote in his journal, "I felt my heart strangely warmed."[1] The faith he had studied, believed, and taught with his head became a transforming fire in his heart.

It's not as if Wesley was making this stuff up. He found the idea of the transformation of the heart rooted deeply in Scripture and Christian tradition. He heard it in God's promise to the Old Testament prophet Ezekiel: "I will give you a new heart and put a new spirit in you. I will remove your stony heart from your body and replace it with a living one" (Ezekiel 36:26).

He learned it from Jesus, who told his followers, "The good person out of the good treasure of the heart produces good, and the evil person out of evil treasure produces evil; for it is out of the abundance of the heart that the mouth speaks" (Luke 6:45 NRSV).

He prayed it regularly in worship using the words of the Book of Common Prayer: "Almighty God, unto whom all hearts are open, all desires known, and from whom no secrets are hid; Cleanse the thoughts of our hearts by the inspiration of thy Holy Spirit that we may perfectly love thee, and worthily magnify thy holy Name, through Christ our Lord. *Amen*."[2]

The word *heart* appears over nine hundred times in the New Revised Standard Version of the Bible. You could describe the Bible as a divinely inspired, spiritual electrocardiogram in which the heart is understood as the life-giving core of our being—the inner source of energy and direction. It is the "mission control center" that determines our desires, fires our passions, frames our values, and energizes our will. That's why the Old Testament writer instructs "keep your heart with all vigilance, / for from it flow the springs of life" (Proverbs 4:23 NRSV).

A Lifelong Journey

Wesley also discovered that God's heart-transforming work is not a static or stationary thing. We do not "get saved" and then sit around waiting to go to heaven. Discipleship in the Methodist tradition is always going somewhere. Salvation is a lifelong journey of heart transformation by which the Spirit of God is at work to form us into people who love God with our whole heart, soul, mind, and strength and who love others as we have been loved by God.

> O for a heart to praise my God,
> A heart from sin set free …
> A heart in every thought renewed
> And full of love divine,
> Perfect and right and pure and good,
> A copy, Lord, of thine.[3]
> —Charles Wesley

Wesley called this process of heart transformation "Christian perfection" or "being made perfect in love." He identified it as "the grand *depositum* which God has lodged with the people called Methodists" and saw it as God's mission for the early Methodists.[4] He called them to a methodical practice of spiritual disciplines and service through which the Spirit of God would be at work in their lives to restore the image of God within, to renew their hearts in love for God and love for others, and to empower them to become the agents of God's transformation in the world.

This study attempts to reclaim Wesley's understanding of "Christian perfection" with the goal of equipping you and those journeying with you to continue to grow into the likeness of God's love in Christ and to become the living expression of that love in the world.

A Group Experience

This workbook can be used as a guide to individual spiritual growth. But because ongoing growth in discipleship is best accomplished in community and because that kind of small group experience is at the heart of the Wesleyan tradition, *A Disciple's Heart* is designed for use primarily in a small group and, if desired, a congregation-wide emphasis. Three resources facilitate the journey.

Daily Workbook

This *Daily Workbook* is designed to foster personal spiritual growth as you develop your own pattern of daily Scripture reading, prayer, and personal reflection through five daily readings for each week. You are invited to journal your own reflections in response to guided questions as well as define your own next steps for growth. You will have the opportunity to share your personal discoveries with your small group as you learn and grow together in community.

The practice of daily spiritual discipline and personal journaling is patterned after the practice of the first Methodists at Oxford University in the eighteenth century. One of our companions along the way is Benjamin Ingham (1712–1772), whose journal gives us direct access to the way Wesley's first followers entered into what they called "holy living."[5] Like these early Methodists, you will be encouraged to reflect on your personal growth in the context of your own current relationships and experiences.

Companion Reader

The *Companion Reader* provides background and deeper understanding of each week's theme from a distinctly Wesleyan perspective. It also includes recommendations for continued study that can be used for your ongoing development. Whether you are a group member or the leader of your group, you will find this to be a valuable resource for enhancing your journey.

Leader Guide

A separate *Leader Guide* provides facilitators with tips for leading a group, six ready-to-use session guides, and ideas for using *A Disciple's Heart* in a congregation-wide focus. Free downloadable leader helps such as sample e-mails, handouts, and PowerPoints are also available.

Remember that being made perfect in love is not a "pull-yourself-up-by-your-bootstraps" project. John Wesley would want us to be clear that it is always and only a work of God's grace in the human heart through the power of the Holy Spirit. It is, however, a work of the Spirit in which we are active participants, not passive observers. In the words of the Apostle Paul, we are called to "work out [our] own salvation with fear and trembling; for it is God who is at work in [us], enabling [us] to will and to work for his good pleasure" (Philippians 2:12-13 NRSV).

These words from one of Charles Wesley's best-loved hymns describe the end toward which our discipleship is moving. May they become your own personal prayer as you commit yourself to pursuing a disciple's heart:

> Finish, then, thy new creation;
> Pure and spotless let us be.
> Let us see thy great salvation
> Perfectly restored in thee;
> Changed from glory into glory,
> Till in heaven we take our place,
> Till we cast our crowns before thee,
> Lost in wonder, love, and praise.[6]

A Disciple's Heart: Daily Workbook

AN OVERVIEW OF *A DISCIPLE'S PATH*

A Disciple's Path, our previous study, is designed to help churches be more intentional in helping people to become disciples of Jesus Christ and to grow in discipleship. It lays a foundation for this resource. Though it is not necessary to complete *A Disciple's Path* prior to beginning this study, it can serve as a helpful first step or refresher course for the journey of discipleship.

A Disciple's Path uses a framework that

- is rooted in our Wesleyan heritage yet is fully compatible with a diverse congregation,
- emphasizes growth in a relationship with Christ,
- acknowledges that our next steps for growth may not look the same, and
- focuses on practices of spiritual discipline rather than programs as a means of measuring discipleship growth.

Rather than a one-size-fits-all approach, it meets seekers, newcomers, and long-term followers of the faith right where they are and invites them to take their next appropriate step to grow their relationship with Christ and the church—moving out from individual salvation to participation in God's transformation of the world.

The discipleship pathway is built around five essential elements.

1. Understand the definition of *disciple*.

What is a *disciple*? Not everyone has a shared definition of *disciple*. When we began to search the Scriptures for a definition, we were drawn to the great commandment in Luke 10:25-28. Based on Jesus' words, we defined a disciple this way:

Disciple – a follower of Jesus whose life is *centering* on loving God and loving others

As the first four words make clear, this definition is grounded in following Jesus. We are drawn to his teaching and believe who the Scriptures and the church say that he is. Being a disciple involves a growing trust in him for salvation. Let's be honest, we are not going to follow a person or God whose character we don't know or believe in.

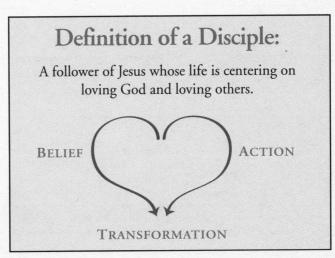

Definition of a Disciple:

A follower of Jesus whose life is centering on loving God and loving others.

BELIEF ACTION

TRANSFORMATION

But is belief enough to be considered a "follower of Jesus"? The word *follow* implies something that is done with your feet, not just with "right thoughts" in your head.

The second part of the definition, "whose life is centering on loving God and loving others," indicates that action is required in order to follow Jesus. We use the present participle *centering* rather than the past tense *centered* because the faith journey is an ongoing process that never ends while we are on this earth. Sometimes belief is enough to change action. Other times action is what initiates or deepens belief. But when they work together, the miracle of transformation happens. In other words, a disciple is one who believes in Jesus' life, death, and resurrection and is actively engaged in making his love a reality in this world.

2. Learn the relationship stages of growth.

Once we have a shared definition of *disciple*, we can identify where we are in relationship with Christ. We have categorized these stages in terms of relationship—strangers, acquaintances, friends, good friends, and intimate friends.

These are broad categories that give us an idea of what our relationship with Jesus might look like as we grow. As we move from strangers to intimate friends, we spend more time, have deeper commitment, and become more vulnerable. These stages are not rigid but flexible and fluid.

The faith journey, like any journey, is filled with twists and turns along the way. The purpose of identifying where you are in relationship to Christ is to give you an idea of where you are now so that you can begin to identify what your next steps might be as you continually move more deeply

---

Relationship Stages

As we grow in relationship with Jesus, different stages might look like this:

Ignoring	Exploring	Getting Started	Going Deeper	Centering
(Strangers)	(Acquaintances)	(Friends)	(Good Friends)	(Intimate Friends)
"I don't know if I believe in God." "I believe in God, but I don't need a faith community."	"I believe in God, but I'm not sure about Jesus or the church." "My faith is not a significant part of my life."	"I believe in Jesus, and I am working on what it means to follow him." "I am participating in the life of the church."	"My relationship with Jesus makes a difference in how I live my life. I am discovering how my life can make God's love real in the world."	"Following Jesus is the most important thing in my life." "My life is part of God's transformation of the world."

Prevenient   Justifying   Sanctifying

We experience God's grace in new ways as we grow in relationship with Jesus.

A Disciple's Heart: Daily Workbook

into life that is centering on Christ. Striving to move toward intimate friendship with Christ is the call for all disciples. It begs the question, *How do we move from being strangers to intimate friends?*

3. Understand grace and the unique roles that God, the church and family, and the individual play in spiritual growth.

When it comes to spiritual growth, the good news is that the individual isn't called to do it alone! God, the church and family, and the individual each have a role to play. These elements work together to help us to grow as disciples so that we may become intimate friends with Christ.

Wesleyan theology is grounded in the belief that faith formation occurs through the partnership of God's action and human action. God's grace works within persons to deepen their relationship with Christ through participating in the life of the faith community, which leads them to respond to the enabling work of the Holy Spirit in faithful Christian living.

God initiates and sustains the whole process of faith through grace—prevenient (preventing), justifying, and sanctifying grace. God calls and is drawing all people, regardless of where they are in their relationship with God, into a closer love relationship.

The church and family nurture, encourage, and challenge individuals as they grow. This is done primarily through community spiritual practices of corporate worship, small group community, and gifts-based service in the church and out in the world.

The individual's role is to respond to the opportunities provided by the church and to engage in personal spiritual disciplines.

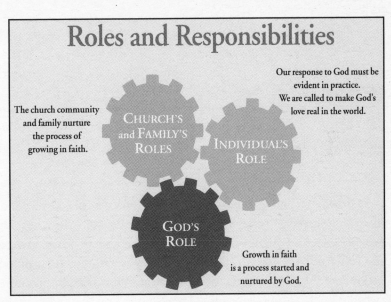

Roles and Responsibilities

The church community and family nurture the process of growing in faith.

CHURCH'S and FAMILY'S ROLES

INDIVIDUAL'S ROLE

Our response to God must be evident in practice. We are called to make God's love real in the world.

GOD'S ROLE

Growth in faith is a process started and nurtured by God.

4. Recognize that spiritual practices are what nurture our relationship with God, and that they look different as we grow.

This essential element of *A Disciple's Path* recognizes that God is never through with us. Through spiritual practices or disciplines, we continually nurture and grow our relationship with God. The essential practices are prayer and meditation, Scripture reflection, financial generosity, and invitational evangelism. Each of these practices is an expression of loving God and/or of loving others. Through these practices God changes us, and as we change, the ways in which we engage in these disciplines should also change.

The following chart gives us an idea of how these practices can change.

Spiritual Practices Change as We Grow

	Exploring	Getting Started	Going Deeper	Centering
PERSONAL SPIRITUAL DISCIPLINES – to do on my own				
PRAYER and	Formal prayers Grace before meals Lord's Prayer	Informal prayers Develop regular time/place Pray with a small group	Conversational prayer Learn different types of prayer	Contemplative prayer Silent prayer Fasting
SCRIPTURE MEDITATION	Bible reading for knowledge and understanding	Follow daily Bible readings Read Bible for comfort and inspiration	Bible reading and reflection for transformation	Bible reading (daily) Bible reflection (daily) Lectio Divina
FINANCIAL GENEROSITY	Occasional giving	Regular giving	Tithing	Sacrificial generosity beyond the tithe
INVITATIONAL EVANGELISM	Explore questions about Jesus Christ	Get to know the gospel story and your story	Find opportunities to share your witness	Help others share their witness
CHRISTIAN COMMUNITY – to do with others				
SMALL-GROUP COMMUNITY	Newcomer class Low-commitment group Exploring faith class	Short-term class Bible study group Sunday school	Relationship-focused group (for accountability, fellowship, Bible study, service, and prayer) Long-term Bible study	Guided by spiritual mentor Lead others in small-group covenant group Discipleship accountability group
CORPORATE WORSHIP	Occasional participation in worship and Communion	Familiarity with elements of corporate worship and Communion	Transformative participation in worship and Communion	Experience the significance and power of corporate worship and Communion
GIFTS-BASED SERVICE	Serve where needed	Discover your spiritual gifts and serve out of giftedness	Discern God's call	Live out God's call and equip others to serve

Growing in one spiritual practice doesn't necessarily correspond with growth in other areas. You can be exploring one practice while going deeper in another. And of course, growth in these practices does not necessarily correspond with growth in what we believe. Sometimes we change our belief and one of these practices changes as a result. Other times we begin with changing our actions, and through the practice of these spiritual disciplines our beliefs are changed. Growth is never as linear as this chart might suggest.

The discipleship path is seldom a straight line. There even may be times of regression. The important thing is to keep following Jesus on the path. Wherever you are right now with each practice is good, but it is not where you are supposed to stay indefinitely.

5. Join with the church to participate in God's transformation of the world.

The final essential affirms that individually and communally we are part of God's plan of transformation—part of God bringing the kingdom of God to earth here and now.

A Disciple's Heart: Daily Workbook

We said that God is responsible for any spiritual growth. God calls us into relationship with Jesus, and we respond. As we follow and grow in the spiritual practices (both as individuals and as a faith community), God moves us more deeply into loving God and loving others.

This chart illustrates that as we follow Jesus and move to a life that is centering in loving God and loving others through our beliefs and actions (the arrows pointing in), the Holy Spirit transforms our hearts. Transformed hearts result in lives that are focused outwardly and are actively involved in God's transformation of the world (the arrows pointing out). This outward movement becomes bigger than anything you could do on your own. Spiritual growth is never just about you but about the whole body of Christ. When the community grows together, amazing things happen.

God uses our response in his redeeming and transforming work. As we grow together, lives are transformed, Christian community is created, and the world around us is healed. This is all part of God's plan of salvation and redemption, and each one of us has an important part to play.

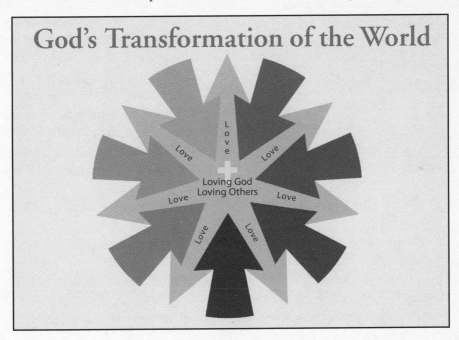

The responses to *A Disciple's Path* from individuals and congregations across the nation have confirmed the way the Spirit of God continues to use these time-tested disciplines in the Wesleyan tradition to transform lives, build Christian community, and engage growing disciples in God's transformation of the world. Welcome to the disciple's path!

WEEK 1
WHERE DO WE GO FROM HERE?

In *A Disciple's Path* we defined a disciple as "a follower of Jesus Christ whose life is centering on loving God and loving others."[1] The continuing present tense indicates that discipleship is an ongoing process of continued growth through which we are becoming more and more clearly centered in our commitment to Christ. Having made that directional decision, the question becomes *Where do we go from here?* In other words, what is the direction or goal or end toward which the journey of discipleship is taking us?

> Thy nature, gracious Lord, impart,
>   Come quickly from above;
> Write thy new name upon my heart,
>   Thy new, best name of Love.[2]
> —Charles Wesley

Benjamin Ingham was searching for that sense of direction early one morning when he made his way through Oxford to John Wesley's apartment at Lincoln College in the spring of 1734. Ingham was drawn to Wesley out of an unrelenting desire for a "holy" life. He was looking for practical ways to develop a richer, deeper, more faithful life as a follower of Jesus Christ. Under Wesley's guidance, Ingham was drawn into a small group with a few other students who met weekly to encourage each other's faith, to hold each other accountable to their spiritual disciplines, and to serve the needs of the poor.

Ingham's journal models the defining elements of discipleship in the Wesleyan tradition.

- It begins as a response to a gnawing, soul-level hunger for a closer relationship with God.
- It involves a personal commitment to become a more faithful follower of Jesus Christ.
- It is formed by specific spiritual and personal disciplines through which the Spirit of God can be at work to continually form us into the likeness of Christ.
- It is lived in community with other disciples who encourage our growth and hold us accountable to our spiritual disciplines.
- It moves us into the world in loving service to others, particularly to people in need.

This week we will discover how the disciplines that enabled the spiritual growth of the early Methodists at Oxford can become practical tools by which the love of God revealed in Jesus transforms our hearts into the likeness of Christ.

WEEK 1: DAY 1
WHAT ARE YOU LOOKING FOR?

Scripture Readings

Read John 1:35-42 and Mark 1:16-20.

Today's Message

Everyone who goes fishing has his or her own fishing story. I remember meeting my son-in-law's ninety-something-year-old grandmother, who lived her entire life along the river in the low country of South Carolina. She was a tiny little woman who grabbed my hand with a stronger grip than I expected and showed no intention of letting go. I said, "I hear you like to fish." She looked me straight in the eye and said, "Yep. And I think I hooked a big one this time." It was her way of welcoming me into the family.

All four Gospel writers—Matthew, Mark, Luke, and John—tell the story of Jesus and the fishermen. But like most fishing stories, each one has his own way of telling it.

In Mark's Gospel, Jesus finds Simon and Andrew casting their nets into the sea because, after all, they were fishermen (Mark 1:16). What else would you expect them to be doing? "Fishermen" defined who they were. "Casting their nets" was their profession. It described what they did to make a living. It was the ordinary pattern of their ordinary lives. Jesus shows up as an unexpected intrusion into their ordinary, net-casting, fish-catching lives. But it turns out that Jesus is the fisherman casting the net this time. He offers them an extraordinary invitation that would change the direction of their lives.

"Come, follow me," he said, "and I'll show you how to fish for people." It was an offer they couldn't refuse. For reasons they probably could never explain, "Right away, they left their nets and followed him" (Mark 1:17-18). Jesus hooked two other fishermen named James and John the same way.

John's version begins with two "spiritual seekers" who have been listening to the preaching of John the Baptist. Dissatisfied with the way life is, they are casting their nets to find a richer, deeper, fuller life in relationship with God. I've known people like them in every community I've served. They are honest skeptics who are not satisfied with simplistic answers to complex questions. They are searching for a faith that makes sense in their brains even as it makes a difference in their hearts.

Jesus greets them with a question. "What are you looking for?" (John 1:38). They say they are looking for a rabbi, a teacher, someone to show them the way to live in a new relationship with God. Jesus offers the invitation, "Come and see." John says, "So they went and saw" (1:39). In fact, they spend the entire day checking Jesus out. At the end of the day, Andrew runs off to tell his brother, Simon, that he has found what he was looking for, and he invites Simon to come and see for himself.

Same fishermen. Different stories. Our tendency is to call out the fact checkers to find out which version got it exactly right, but that's not a question the Gospel writers have any interest in answering. There was no attempt to merge them into one event. They hang both stories out there as if to say, "This is how people meet Jesus."

Sometimes Jesus finds us. He shows up as an unexpected intrusion into our ordinary, busy lives. But we somehow know that if we pass up the invitation to follow him, we will miss out on one of the most important opportunities that ever came our way. It's a lot like falling in love. Sometimes it happens unexpectedly when a special person steps into our lives.

> I sought the Lord, and afterward I knew
> He moved my soul to seek him, seeking me.
> It was not I that found, O Savior true;
> No, I was found of thee.[3]

Others find Jesus through an arduous search. Dissatisfied with the way life is, we are looking for something more. During a time of spiritual exploration, we receive the same invitation, "Come and see." We read the story and check out the evidence for ourselves. Along the way we discover in the words, life, death, and resurrection of Jesus the one for whom we had always been searching. We discover that Jesus has been what Francis Thompson called "The Hound of Heaven" who was searching for us long before we began searching for him.

However the invitation comes, the decisive moments are those times when we make a commitment to leave our old nets behind and take the next appropriate step in following him. We turn from our past and choose to follow Jesus, not because we know all the answers to all our questions but because we know that he is the one who can lead us toward the answers—that he is the one worth following. We commit all that we know of ourselves to all that we know of Christ, knowing that we still have a lot to learn. The Gospels call this experience *repentance*. The word literally means to turn in a new direction.

That's when God's work of heart transformation begins. One of the words we use to describe that change is *conversion*. Like shifting from using a PC to a Mac, it involves a conversion from one operating platform to another. Jesus expresses this change with a Greek play on words when he tells the fishermen that he will show them how to fish for people. Instead of casting their nets for grouper, crabs, or mahi-mahi, they will be casting their nets for other people who will follow them as they follow Jesus. At the beginning of his ministry, Jesus establishes the pattern. People become disciples because other disciples disciple them.

Don't miss the unique way in which Jesus frames the invitation to discipleship in a way that is custom-made for whom these fishermen are. In the same way, Jesus meets Matthew, the tax collector, at his workplace and offers the same invitation, "Follow me." Matthew leaves his old career behind. That evening, we find Jesus having dinner with Matthew's disreputable, irreligious coworkers and friends. Matthew was able to introduce Jesus to a crowd of people the fishermen never could have reached (Matthew 9:9-13).

A Disciple's Heart: Daily Workbook

In the same way, the Risen Christ meets us in the very real places of our very ordinary lives. He calls us to leave behind our old ways of thinking and living in order to turn in a new direction. Then he takes the uniqueness of who we are and what we have to offer and uses us to invite others to follow us as we follow him.

Whoever you are, wherever you've been, whatever you do for a living, whatever you believe or don't believe, the invitation is always the same. We are called to follow Jesus and allow him to transform our lives into the kind of life he lived so that others will see his life in us and follow him.

Your Reflections

- Where do you find yourself in the Scripture Readings? Which character most closely matches your experience with Christ?

  I have always identified as the disciple John because I joined the Christian Church early & was baptized

- What are the things that you have had to leave behind because of your relationship with Christ and the church?

  Pursuit of wealth

- What are the "nets" to which you still cling?

  I am an introvert & find it hard to go out invite strangers to church

- How are you fishing for people? How do you invite people to experience the love of God in Christ?

  I try to do it by example

Your Guide to Prayer and Action

God, I give thanks for your ever-present invitation and for the grace that preceded my decision to respond to your invitation. I pray now that I might invite you into the area of my life that most needs your presence. If I am holding on to a net that prevents me from loving you or loving others, give me the strength to let it go so that I could be more effective in being a fisher of people. Amen.

- Think of a person who is in your life who currently doesn't appear to have a life committed to God. Pray for this person by name throughout the day.
- Pray through Mark 1:16-20 using *Lectio Divina*, an ancient practice of prayerful meditation of Scripture in which you listen to what Christ has to say. Follow the steps on page 119. Whatever word or phrase God gives you during this time, use it throughout the day to center your thoughts.

My daughter

John 6:26-27

"Work for the food that last for eternal life"

WEEK 1: DAY 2
WHAT KIND OF PERFECTION ARE YOU AIMING FOR?

Scripture Reading

Read Matthew 5:43-48.

Today's Message

Are you going on to perfection?
Do you expect to be made perfect in love in this life?
Are you earnestly striving after perfection in love?[4]

In the Methodist tradition, these three questions are asked of persons who are entering into the ordained ministry, but they also could be asked of every follower of Christ. They go to the heart of the journey of discipleship and invite each of us into lifelong practices of discipleship that enable us to be formed into followers of Jesus whose lives are centering in loving God and loving others. They lure us into an ongoing process of heart transformation that continues throughout our lives.

Jesus' words in the Sermon on the Mount are even more daunting than Wesley's ordination questions. It must have been just as disturbing for his first disciples as it is for us to hear him say, "Be perfect, therefore, as your heavenly Father is perfect" (Matthew 5:48 NRSV).

If we apply our current culture's ideas of "perfection" to Jesus' words, we could end up with a neurotic form of perfectionism that is utterly impossible to attain and can lead to destructive personality traits, unhealthy ambition, and broken relationships. We might imagine the perfection of an Olympic ice skater with points being deducted for every minute flaw in his or her performance.

In the New Testament, the word *perfection* comes from the Greek word *teleios*, meaning "complete" or "whole."[5] Perfection is the end or goal toward which all things are moving. *Perfection* can also mean "entire," "mature," or "full-grown." Kathleen Norris says that perfection as Jesus defines it means "to make room for growth, for the changes that bring us to maturity, to ripeness."[6]

In the context of the Sermon on the Mount, perfection is neither the faultless fulfillment of an external set of rules and regulations nor our rational ascent to a perfectly comprehended concept or doctrine. Rather, it is God's way of love being worked out in human relationships. It is gracious hospitality to the presence of the living Christ settling into our hearts, taking up residence in our relationships, and taking control of every area of our lives.

Jesus defines "perfection" as loving others the way that God loves us (Matthew 5:43-47). He describes the radical uniqueness of this way of love by calling his disciples to love their enemies and to pray for those who persecute them. It is the universal love God demonstrates in making the sun shine on both the evil and the good and by making rain fall on both the righteous and the unrighteous (Matthew 5:45). Perfection is the fulfillment of the commandment to love God with our whole heart, soul, mind, and strength, and to love others as we have been loved by God (Luke 10:27; John 13:34).

> Come quickly, then, my Lord, and take
> Possession of Thine own;
> My longing heart vouchsafe to make
> Thine everlasting throne.
>
> Assert Thy claim, receive Thy right,
> Come quickly from above,
> And sink me to perfection's height,
> The depth of humble love. [7]
> –Charles Wesley

For disciples in the Wesleyan tradition, the aim of the Christian life is for the love of God that came among us in Jesus to take up residence in every area of our lives so that we become the agents of God's transforming love at work in the world.

My homegrown definition of Christian perfection is that it is what happens in our lives when God's Spirit takes control of our attitudes, values, commitments, relationships, and loyalties so that we are increasingly motivated, led, and directed by nothing less than the love that became flesh among us in Jesus Christ. It is the love of Christ purifying our motives, refining our desires, liberating our spirit, and empowering our actions. It is what the Apostle Paul intended when he prayed that "Christ will live in your hearts through faith. As a result of having strong roots in love, I ask that you'll have the power to grasp love's width and length, height and depth, together with all believers. I ask that you'll know the love of Christ that is beyond knowledge so that you will be filled entirely with the fullness of God" (Ephesians 3:17-19).

Wesley pushed back on the critics who questioned his message of Christian perfection with questions that continue to challenge us today:

> By Christian perfection I mean loving God with all our heart. Do you object to this? I mean a heart and life all devoted to God. Do you desire less? . . . I mean having all the mind that was in Christ. Is this going too far? [8]

So, here's the question for each of us: If you aren't going on toward perfection, then where are you are going? Why would you want to go in any other direction?

Your Reflections
- Reflect on the three questions...
  o Are you going on to perfection? Is your deepest desire for the love of God to take up residence in every area of your life?

A Disciple's Heart: Daily Workbook

- o Do you expect to be made perfect in love in this life (to love others the way that God loves you)?
- o Are you earnestly striving after perfection in love?

- What is the difference between the perfection Wesley described and the way perfection is portrayed in our culture? Are there any similarities?

The difference is that the world has a narsistic goal to be better than others. God wants us to love other rather than self.

- How has your love grown as you have matured? Name some tangible signs that your love is being made complete in your relationships.

I have become more focused on my family & friends

- What attitudes or dispositions are inhibiting you from growing toward greater maturity in Christ? What action can you take to offer those attitudes to Christ so that he may reshape them?

I still spend too much time worrying about finances & tempory things like my house

Your Guide to Prayer and Action

Loving God, shape and mold me, my family, my friends, and my faith community into a more complete kind of love. Illuminate any dispositions or attitudes that will prevent us from the Great Commandment of loving with our whole heart, mind, soul, and strength, and shape us into who we really are made to be. Amen.

- Use *Lectio Divina* to pray through Matthew 5:43-48 (refer to the steps on page 119). Use the word or phrase God gives you during this time throughout the day to center your thoughts.
- Identify one attitude or disposition of which you are aware that is holding you back from a more robust and mature love of God and others.
- o Ask God to enter into your unwillingness to let it go.
- o Find a Scripture that counters the attitude. Say it throughout the day.
- o Share the attitude and Scripture with a trusted friend, an accountability partner, or a spiritual guide/director.

Week 1: Day 3
Who Really Wants to Be Holy?

Scripture Reading

Read 1 Peter 1:13-16.

Today's Message

What image or picture comes to mind when you think of someone who is "holy"? Some might recall former "Saturday Night Live" cast member Dana Carvey's classic portrayal of "The Church Lady," who looked down her pretentiously pious nose and snarled at her talk show guests with her judgmental "holier-than-thou" attitude.

Unfortunately, that's the kind of image many young adults have of people who claim to be Christians today. A recent study of young adults between the ages of sixteen and twenty-nine found that among non-Christians, nine out of the top twelve perceptions were negative. The two most common were that Christians are judgmental (87 percent) and hypocritical (85 percent).[10] Self-righteous, pretentiously pious, arrogant, and mean-spirited people who masquerade as Christians have created a narrow and negative impression of what it means to be holy.

Negative cultural images are enough to make many of us question whether we really want to be "holy." Yet it was a desire to live a "holy life" that gave birth to the Methodist movement among students at Oxford, England, in the eighteenth century.

In spite of negative cultural perceptions of holiness, my sense is that when people experience genuine holiness in the life of another person, there is an unmistakable attraction to it. One person living a grace-filled life can undermine the negative impressions that are so apparent in the world around us. The world's fascination with Pope Francis, for example, demonstrates the way one person whose life reflects the life of Jesus can impact the lives of others.

In today's Scripture, the writer of the epistle reaches back to the Old Testament book of Leviticus to remind followers of Christ of the timeless call to be holy as God is holy (Leviticus 11:14). Eugene Peterson captured the energy and direction of the text when he paraphrased the epistle to read: "As obedient children, let yourselves be pulled into a way of life shaped by God's life, a life energetic and blazing with holiness. God said, 'I am holy; you be holy'" (1 Peter 1:13-16 *The Message*). Holiness is nothing less than the invitation to experience in our finite existence the fullness of the love and life of the infinite God.

The Wesleyan understanding of holiness points in two directions at the same time. "Holiness of heart" is the inward work of the Spirit that draws us deeper into loving God. "Holiness of life" is the outward work of the Spirit by which we grow in our love of others and become the agents of God's love in the world. It is what life looks like when we say yes to the heart-transforming presence of the Spirit of Christ in our lives.

Today's Scripture Reading also calls us to action—to prepare our minds, discipline ourselves, and refuse to be controlled by the passions and desires of our old way of living. We are active participants in the process. Our growth in holiness results from a combination of receptivity to the work of the Holy Spirit and disciplined action that brings our lives into harmony with the holiness we seek.

One of the ways we have attempted to encourage people in our congregation to grow in this understanding of holiness is to ask these questions: Are you more like Jesus today than you were six months or a year ago? Are you more alive to the presence of God, more loving, more compassionate, more hopeful than you were when you started following Jesus? If not, why not?

The "Church Lady" got it wrong. Holiness is not about being "holier than thou." It's about becoming more like Jesus than we ever imagined we could be.

> "With each new 'Yes' [Mother Teresa] emerged more intimately united with the Lord to whom she was ready to give 'even life itself.'"[11]
> —Brian Kolodiejchuk

Your Reflections

- What desires or passions in your past or present are drawing you away from being holy?

  Watching too much junk TV Sports, movies, news

- How do you prepare yourself to love God and others each day? Are there habits or practices that help to prepare your mind and thoughts?

  I try to plan how best use my time I pray in the evening to do better the next day

- Who comes to mind when you think of being "holy"? List the attitudes, behaviors, and actions that demonstrate this person's inward and outward (heart and life) holiness. How does he or she love others and/or promote social change?

  My Aunt Vesta & Evelyn Moore
  They both read their bibles,
  prayed & care about others.

- How does supporting, encouraging, and engaging with others, particularly the marginalized, make us holy—more like Christ?

  It helps us understand their problems
  and makes us care about them
  & guides us to help them as
  Christ would

Your Guide to Prayer and Action

Holy God, I come in gratitude for your goodness, your holiness, and your call to be perfect even though it feels overwhelming and, at times, impossible. If there are passions or desires that are drawing me away from holiness, I pray for your intervention. Infuse my thoughts with your sanctifying love, and develop my character so that I may live this day in obedience to you. Amen.

- Review your calendar or schedule for the day. Pray for each appointment or scheduled interaction. Consider how you can be more like Jesus today.
- Meditate on the meaning of holiness. Ask God to show you how you can become more like Jesus today.
- Use *Lectio Divina* to pray through 1 Peter 1:13-16 (refer to the steps on page 119). Use the word or phrase God gives you during this time throughout the day to center your thoughts.

A Disciple's Heart: Daily Workbook

Week 1: Day 4
The Disciplines that Shape Us

Scripture Reading

Read 1 Corinthians 9:24-27.

Today's Message

Did you make any New Year's resolutions this year? How successful have you been at keeping those resolutions?

It happens every year. As the clock counts down to midnight, we make all sorts of resolutions for the year ahead. One thing the resolutions have in common is that they point us in the direction of a better life. No one resolves to get less exercise, fail in a career, or become a meaner person.

But as most of us have discovered, it's easier to make resolutions than to keep them. A lot of folks who show up at the gym in January won't be there come March. The kind of change that really matters doesn't just happen. It always requires disciplined action. It grows out of small changes that, if practiced over time, result in significant change in the way we think and live. Only practice makes perfect.

In his first letter to the church in Corinth, Paul describes his own life of discipleship in terms that any athlete can understand. He compares himself to runners preparing for the Olympics who discipline themselves for the sake of the prize that is before them.

John Ortberg uses that same metaphor when he makes a helpful distinction between "trying" and "training." He says that anyone can try to run a marathon, but the only people who will actually accomplish it are those who train for it.[12] By training, we are able to accomplish things that would never be possible if we merely tried.

In the same way, anyone can make a resolution to be more loving, more faithful, more gracious, more tolerant—in a word, more like Jesus. Anyone can try to be more holy. But the only people who actually experience the holy life are those who train for it by organizing their lives around specific disciplines that, if practiced over time, result in genuine transformation.

I grew up in the "holiness" branch of the Methodist tradition, which included attending an old-fashioned Methodist "camp meeting" every summer. The singing was robust, the sermons were powerful, and every service concluded with a passionate invitation to "come forward" to a place of prayer and experience God's transformation of our lives. Preachers described "entire sanctification" as a "second work of grace" in which sin would be eradicated from our lives. I made my way to that altar over and over again, looking for that kind of overwhelming spiritual experience.

The permanent gift for my life from that tradition is that I learned along the way that whenever I feel the tug of the Spirit in my heart, the only appropriate response is to say yes. The negative

> "O, begin! Fix some part of every day for private exercises…Whether you like it or no, read and pray daily. …Do justice to your own soul; give it time and means to grow. Do not starve yourselves any longer."[13]
> —John Wesley

side of the tradition is that I kept looking for one dramatic moment of transformation that would settle every struggle in my adolescent soul. I've learned across the years that while the need for spiritual change may be inspired in a moment, genuine heart transformation takes a lifetime. It is always the result of the Spirit of God at work through the time-tested disciplines that have transformed the lives of people across the generations—and that continue to transform hearts and lives today.

Wesley's followers at Oxford were mockingly called Methodists because they were so persistently methodical in the way they applied the spiritual disciplines to every area of their lives. We know what those practices are. They are the biblically rooted disciplines by which the Spirit of God is at work in our hearts to shape us into people who love God with all our heart, soul, mind, and strength and who love others the way we have been loved by God. Although they can be organized in different ways, they always include:

Prayer
Scripture reflection
Corporate worship
Small group community
Gifts-based service
Financial generosity
Invitational evangelism

In *A Disciple's Path*, we organized these practices around the way members of The United Methodist Church commit themselves to a life of prayer, presence, gifts, service, and witness. Regardless of our denominational affiliation, these are the disciplines that, if practiced over time, enable us to become the kind of people we believe God has created, called, and redeemed us to become. They are the practices by which we grow in holiness and move toward Christian perfection.

Your Reflections

- Do you consider yourself to be in strict training spiritually? Why or why not?

Getting there but always to go

- Remember a time with regard to your spiritual "training" when you were most disciplined. What motivated you? What worked? What didn't?

  Mission trips, Reach WC, Habitat Service w others, working toward a goal

- Which of the spiritual practices listed above come easier to you? Which are more challenging?

  Small group, service

  Invitational evangelism

Your Guide to Prayer and Action

Lord God, I realize the race of life requires training—training that cultivates a deeper relationship with you. Prepare me for the joys and challenges that I am experiencing now and will face in the future. Give me the discipline to engage in the practices that you will use to prepare me for the prize you have for me. In Christ's name I pray. Amen.

- Training is best done with a partner. If you don't have a spiritual accountability partner, identify someone you could invite to join you in a deeper "spiritual training regimen." It is recommended that you find a discipleship partner of the same gender.

  Partner John or Jim T
  Joe

- Explore small group opportunities in your church or community, such as "covenant groups" or accountability groups.
- Use *Lectio Divina* to pray through 1 Corinthians 9:24-27 (refer to the steps on page 119). Use the word or phrase God gives you during this time throughout the day to center your thoughts.

Week 1: Day 5
An End Without an Ending

Scripture Reading
Read Psalm 84.

Today's Message

When it comes to reading novels, I am a compulsive last page reader. I often sneak a peek at the last page to see where the story comes out in the end.

Sometimes the word *end* means "the end." It is literally the last page, the conclusion, the finale after which nothing else happens. When it refers to the last play of the game, the final frame of a movie, or the end of a dentist appointment, it can be a pleasant conclusion that leads to celebration. If it refers to the end of a relationship, the unexpected end of a career, or the end of a life, it can be painful and lead to sadness.

But the *end* can also name the goal toward which we are constantly moving. It is an unachieved ambition, the illusive vision, the relentless hope or heartfelt desire that persistently draws us toward something that is always beyond us in the future. It defines the goal of continued improvement that never ends.

In our Scripture for today, the psalmist cries out with a heart-level, passionate longing to be in worship in the Temple. I experience the psalm as a visual metaphor for a gnawing, relentless spiritual hunger to live in a deeper, richer, fuller experience of the presence of God. The psalm paints the picture of an end without an ending—the lifelong desire for an intimate relationship with God that never ends.

In the same way, the New Testament lifts before us a desired outcome that never ends. It's the vision of a relationship with God that keeps us moving toward a deeper, richer, more Christ-like life that will ultimately be fulfilled in eternal life with God that will never end. On this side of heaven, Christian perfection—which is being made perfect in love—is also that kind of end without an ending. It's the continuing journey toward a heart that is fully transformed by the love of God in Christ. No matter where we are along the journey of discipleship, there is always a longing for something more.

A simple, country farmer in the rural congregation I served in the early years of my ministry gave me the best definition of Christian perfection that I have ever heard. As we were coming up the church steps early one Sunday morning, I asked, "How are you doing?" He looked me straight in the eye and with a strong sense of determination in his voice he replied, "Well, Preacher, I'm not the man I used to be, and I'm not yet the man I'd like to be, but I'm more the man God wants me to be than I've ever been before." That's good Wesleyan theology!

A Disciple's Heart: Daily Workbook

Christian perfection is an end without an ending toward which we are constantly called to grow throughout this life until God's loving purpose is fulfilled in us in the life to come. That's what Charles Wesley meant when he wrote that we are "Changed from glory into glory / Till in heaven we take our place."[15] Wherever you are in your spiritual journey, the good news is that God always has more love to share, more life to give, and more work to do in your heart in this life and in the life to come.

Your Reflections

- Does your soul long for God in the way that the psalmist describes? If so, describe it in your own words below. If not, why not?

  I strive to live a life full of love of God and of service to his people.

- How have you understood Christian perfection? Reflect on the definitions in today's reading. Which definition resonates with you?

  Living a life that pleases Jesus. The one at the top of the page

- If you could read the last page of the story of your life, how would you want it to read?

  That he lived a life full of love & service to others.

- What might "perfection of love" look like in your life and relationships?

  He was able to reach out to others and draw them closer to God

A Guide to Prayer and Action

God of all beginnings and endings, give us the picture of the end, the hope that you will make us complete. May this be a day that I become more of the person you have called me to be. I ask you to increase my longing for you and my longing to be an instrument of your peace. Amen.

> "How much soever any man has attained, or in how high a degree soever he is perfect, he hath still to 'grow in grace,' and daily to advance in the knowledge and love of God his Savior."[16]
> —John Wesley

- Identify the verse from the Scripture Reading that speaks most to you and write it on a note card or a note in your phone or tablet. Or put it as a reminder that will pop up a few times on your calendar on your phone, tablet, or computer. Recite it throughout your day.
- Pray this prayer:

Wesley Covenant Prayer

I am no longer my own, but thine.
Put me to what thou wilt, rank me with whom thou wilt.
Put me to doing, put me to suffering.
Let me be employed by thee or laid aside for thee,
Exalted for thee or brought low by thee.
Let me be full, let me be empty.
Let me have all things, let me have nothing.
I freely and heartily yield all things
to thy pleasure and disposal.
And now, O glorious and blessed God,
Father, Son, and Holy Spirit,
thou art mine and I am thine. So be it.
And the covenant which I have made on earth,
let it be ratified in heaven. Amen.[17]

WEEK 2
WALKING THE WAY OF SALVATION

"Salvation by Faith" was the title of John Wesley's first sermon after his heart-warming experience at Aldersgate Street. He proclaimed salvation as a present reality, "something attainable, yea, actually attained, on earth, by those who are partakers of this faith."[1] As a result of his heart-warming experience, he was convinced that salvation is not an abstract, theological concept to be believed as much as it is an inward awareness of God's love and grace that makes a tangible difference in the way we live our lives.

William H. Willimon reminds us that salvation is not something we do but something God does. He said that salvation presupposes "that there is something from which we need to be saved, that we are not doing as well as we presume . . . and that the hope for us is not of our devising."[2]

The Hebrew words for *salvation* mean "deliver," "bring to safety," or "redeem." The Greek words mean "rescue," "heal," or "liberate."[3] My working definition is that salvation is God's work of love in the human heart that heals our broken relationships with ourselves, with others, and with God. It is the way God reconciles rebellious human beings to each other and to the God who created them. And it is the way God is at work to set this whole creation free from its bondage to evil, sin, and death.

> "Salvation is God not only reaching out but also specifically reaching down. Jesus makes friends in low places. Some of the lost don't know how lost they are until they get found. Salvation is Jesus getting down on our level, so that we might rise to his."[4]
> —William H. Willimon

Salvation begins in what Wesley called "preventing" or "prevenient" grace. It is our awareness of a hunger for God to do something within us that is beyond our power to create or contain. It is an awareness of our sin and our need for salvation. You could call it a heart disease that needs the healing of a divine cardiologist. From that point on, salvation is a continuing work of God's Spirit in the human heart that persistently calls us to leave old habits, attitudes, and sins behind so that the likeness of Christ can be formed within us.

While there are decisive turning points along the way, being saved is not a one-time event in the past but an ongoing experience of forgiveness and grace through which we grow into holiness. It is the love of God at work in the human heart to shape us into the likeness of Jesus Christ.

This week we explore salvation in the context of Wesley's understanding of grace.

Week 2: Day 1
Whatever Became of Sin?

Scripture Readings
Read Romans 3:22-24 and 5:12-21.

Today's Message

Whatever happened to sin? Does the idea that we are all sinners seem just a little outdated to you? Is it possible that in our contemporary culture we have become complacent about sin?

Whenever we are tempted to become complacent about the reality of sin, the Bible and the daily news headlines remind us of the long, painful story of how things are out of line with God's good purpose for this creation and the seemingly irreparable damage it does to our lives, our relationships, and our environment. When we look squarely at ourselves and our world, we know that sin is still with us.

When speaking of sin, the New Testament uses the Greek word *hamartia*, which means "missing the mark."[5] It's not just referring to individual "sins" but to "sin" as the overall condition of human life that misses the mark of God's intention and is therefore out of alignment with the life-giving purpose of God.

The Bible demonstrates that sin is not just our own, private business. We can't say that it doesn't matter what I do so long as it doesn't hurt someone else. Human life is more interconnected than that. My personal sins are one expression of an overall misalignment of a creation that functions in ways that are out of line with God's design.

But things get worse. There is an aggressive quality to sin. Sin is like a vicious computer virus that infects the whole system. Sin is active rebellion against the loving God who is relentlessly at work to heal, restore, and make things right. Paul reaches back to the Genesis story of the fall (Genesis 3:1-24) to paint a picture of the way sin was passed on with the result that "Just as through one human being sin came into the world, and death came through sin, so death has come to everyone, since everyone has sinned" (Romans 5:12).

And here's the worst part. We're all corrupted by it. That's why Paul says, "There's no distinction. All have sinned and fall short of God's glory" (Romans 3:22-23). That's sin.

But we don't like to admit that we are involved in the business of sin. We'd prefer to keep our brokenness out of plain sight, hidden beneath a comfortable, complacent, Christian facade. Like Adam and Eve trying to hide their nakedness in the garden, we like to pretend that our lives are neatly in line and everything is under control, which, in the end, is a useless attempt to hide behind the fig leaves of our pretentious piety.

But do you remember the end toward which the discipleship journey is taking us? Have we reached perfection? Is every part of our life in perfect alignment with God's purpose? Do we

A Disciple's Heart: Daily Workbook

really love God with our whole heart, soul, mind, and strength—no reservations, no compromises, no hidden selfish agendas? Do we love others, even our enemies, the way we have been loved by God?

If we tell the whole truth, we know what became of sin. It is alive and well within and around us.

Your Reflections

- Where in your life have you been missing the mark? How have you experienced your own evil/sin?

Evangelism is tough for me. Tampa Ecworey too much time

Procrastination I have good ideas but don't always follow thru. The sin of omission

- When is the last time you shared or confessed with another person your sin? *It has been awhile*

- What are the thoughts, attitudes, beliefs, and behaviors you attempt to hide, avoid, or deny? *Stray thoughts, Worries Purient thoughts*

- How do you need to experience a new gift of God's grace and forgiveness?

I need to be more open about my faith

> "Take out the Wesleyan bedrock belief that we are sinners, all the way down, that our sin is pervasive, relentless, and original, and the whole structure of Methodist believing collapses. . . . We don't want ever to lose sight of a prima fact: *We stand in need of redemption.*"[6]
> —William H. Willimon

Your Guide to Prayer and Action

O God, who looks into the deepest corners of my heart, I confess that sometimes I pretend to be better than I am—that I spend more time thinking of my own agendas and desires than striving to discover yours. I fall short and often conceal my separateness from others and from you. Right now I confess my own shortcomings and defects of character. Thank you for forgiving me, for forgiving the church, for forgiving the whole sin-soaked world. May I live in response to your forgiveness in a way that radiates your light. Amen.

- Follow the instructions on page 120 for a time of centering prayer. Read aloud Romans 3:22-24 or 5:12-21 to begin your prayer period, or use another passage of your own choosing.
- If you have not confessed your sin to another person recently (or ever), connect with a pastor, spiritual director, or an accountability partner. If you have no such person, pray that God will send such a person. Identify a next step that you can take to identify or invite a person into this area of your life. (An accountability partner should not be a person to whom you are married or with whom you have an intimate relationship.)

God r

Our faith is a result

A Disciple's Heart: Daily Workbook

WEEK 2: DAY 2
SALVATION IN THREE TENSES

Scripture Reading

Read Romans 5:6-17.

Today's Message

When were you saved?

There was a time when I thought the answer to that question was an event in my personal past. Being "saved" meant that I had responded to an invitation at the conclusion of a powerful sermon in a revival service or at summer camp. It meant that I would "come to the altar" during the singing of multiple verses of "Just As I Am" to confess my sins, receive God's forgiveness, and accept Jesus as my personal Savior. It meant marking a date on the calendar when my life was changed forever.

It happens that way for some people. Some disciples describe their experience as being similar to the way Saul was knocked to the ground on the Damascus Road (Acts 9:1-9). In a dramatic moment, their lives are changed forever. But even Saul's conversion began earlier in his story with the stoning of Stephen (Acts 7:54-8:1) and continued in his visit with Ananias (Acts 9:10-19).

There was a time when I kept looking for that kind of Damascus Road experience of salvation. But two things happened to disrupt my understanding of salvation. First, I discovered that I was making that trip to the altar over and over again. It raised that question of when my salvation actually happened.

The second thing was that I started reading the Bible. The more time I spent with the Scripture, the less I was convinced that being saved was something that happened in a single moment. I began to discover that God's business of salvation involved saving a lot more than just my individual soul. I met Timothy, for whom there was evidently no Damascus Road conversion. Paul told him to "revive God's gift" that had been passed on to him from his mother and grandmother (2 Timothy 1:5-6). That seemed to be the story of my faith too.

One turning point along the way was when I discovered Paul's use of the verbs in his letter to Rome. First, notice the way Paul describes salvation as something that happened in the past. "While we were still weak, at the right moment, Christ died for ungodly people" (Romans 5:6). The "right moment" was a dark Friday afternoon, on a hill outside the city of Jerusalem, when Jesus died on the cross. That's when God's work of salvation was done. We were saved by God's amazing gift of love at the cross.

Paul acknowledges that sometimes in this world a really good person may choose to give his life for the sake of a noble leader or an innocent victim. A Secret Service agent may actually lay down his life for the President; a parent may give his or her life for a child. But have you ever heard of someone offering to take the place of a convicted murderer or a child rapist?

The shock of the gospel is that "God shows his love for us, because while we were still sinners Christ died for us" (Romans 5:8). When we were at our worst, God's love was at its best. The one and only fully, completely good person who ever lived was executed as a criminal, taking into himself all the guilt, suffering, and shame of all our sin. While we were yet sinners, Christ died for ungodly, rebellious, guilty sinners like every one of us.

But Paul doesn't leave the gift of salvation in the past. He declares that "we have peace with God through our Lord Jesus Christ. We have access by faith into this grace in which we stand through him, and we boast in the hope of God's glory" (Romans 5:1-2). Notice that all of the verbs are in the present tense. The salvation that was accomplished on the cross becomes a living reality in our lives right now.

That's what happened for John Wesley at Aldersgate Street. The faith in which he had been raised, the theology he studied and believed in the past, became a present reality in his life. He realized that he did trust in Christ alone for his salvation. He received a deep, inner assurance that God had forgiven his sin and had set him free from the bondage of sin and death.

Salvation doesn't get more present tense than that! What he had believed about God's action in the past had become a "heart-warming" reality in the present. Though he continued to wrestle with his doubts, he had a deep, inner assurance of his present relationship with God.

But Paul doesn't leave it there. He throws our vision out into the future: "If we were reconciled to God through the death of his Son while we were still enemies, now that we have been reconciled, how much more certain is it that we will be saved by his life?" (Romans 5:10-11). We live in the promise of the future fulfillment of God's saving purpose for the whole creation.

Later, Paul compares the whole created order to a woman in labor, groaning in childbirth, longing and waiting for the salvation that was accomplished at the cross to be fulfilled in the whole creation. It leads Paul to the conclusion that "we were saved in hope" (see Romans 8:22-25).

- We **were** saved, reconciled, brought into right relationship with God at the cross. You are a person for whom Jesus died.
- We **are** being saved, justified, made right with God by grace through faith. You can experience God's saving love as a present experience.
- We **will be** saved in the fulfillment of God's saving purpose for the whole creation. You can live with hope in the assurance of that salvation.
- You were saved, you are saved, you will be saved. Salvation is a past, present, and future reality.

A Disciple's Heart: Daily Workbook

Your Reflections

- Describe some of the ways you experience sin in your life as "missing the mark." Then describe some of the ways in which "sin" manifests in the world as the overall condition of human life being out of alignment with God's purpose.

  I fail to reach out to others. There are so many to our country & the world who live with hate in their heart rather than love for one another

- If you had a moment in time when your life was dramatically changed by God's grace, describe it here. If not, describe the process of salvation in your experience.

  When I was baptized in the first Christian Church in Greensburg Ks when I was about ten by a blind minister

- How are you currently experiencing God's saving love in your life?

  My work with Habitat & with my church community

- What is your hope of salvation for the future?

  That we wipe out poverty & hatred

Your Guide to Prayer and Action

Reconciling God, your love has realigned my relationship with you through Jesus' life, death, and resurrection. Warm my heart so that I may live in the state of awareness that Jesus died for me. Connect me to your presence here and now. Amen.

- Follow the instructions on page 120 for a time of centering prayer. Read aloud Romans 5:6-17 to begin your prayer period, or use another passage of your own choosing.
- Pray for a person whom you know is spiritually struggling. Reach out in some way to this person today.

WEEK 2: DAY 3
GRACE ALL THE WAY

Scripture Reading

Read Ephesians 2:1-9.

Today's Message

"Amazing Grace" is one of the best-loved hymns of all time. It was written by a former slave ship captain named John Newton (1725–1807). Under the influence of the Wesleyan revival, he experienced salvation and became an energetic voice for the abolition of slavery in Great Britain. He described his journey of discipleship when he wrote:

> Through many dangers, toils, and snares
> I have already come;
> 'Tis grace that brought me safe thus far,
> and grace will lead me home.[9]

For followers of Christ in the Wesleyan tradition, the way of salvation is the way of grace. It is a journey of grace from beginning to end. It is grace all the way home.

The word *grace* appears more than 225 times in the New Revised Standard Version of the Bible. Paul opened his letter to the Romans with the greeting, "Grace to you and peace from God our Father and the Lord Jesus Christ" (Romans 1:7 NRSV). He told the Ephesians: "For by grace you have been saved through faith, and this is not your own doing; it is the gift of God" (Ephesians 2:8 NRSV).

Here is the definition of grace that we shared in *A Disciple's Path*:

> Grace is the undeserved, unearned, unrepayable gift of the God who loves us enough to meet us where we are, but loves us too much to leave us there. Grace is the love of God at work within us to transform each of our lives into a unique expression of the love of God revealed in Jesus Christ.[10]

Kenneth Cain Kinghorn declared that for Christians in the Wesleyan tradition, "no single word better sums up the message of the Bible than grace."[11]

Wesley gave the Methodists a unique way of seeing salvation as the way of grace. The journey begins with "prevenient" or "preventing" grace. *Prevenient* is probably not a word you used over the breakfast table this morning. It means "that which comes before." It is God's grace at work in our

A Disciple's Heart: Daily Workbook

lives prior to our response. It means that God always gets the first move. God's action is always prior to our response.

The way of salvation leads to "justifying" or "converting" grace. It is God's undeserved love and forgiveness at the cross that makes things right in our relationship with God and draws us into new life in Christ. Many of Charles Wesley's hymns express the shock and surprise of the awareness of God's grace at the cross. None captures it more powerfully and simply than this: "Amazing love! How can it be, / That thou, my God, shouldst die for me!"[13]

But grace doesn't stop there. We don't just get saved and then sit around waiting to go to heaven. The focus of this study is on what Wesley called "sanctifying" grace. It is the continuing process by which the grace of God shapes us into the likeness of Christ all the way from here to heaven.

When I hear folks share their witness of when they were saved and what a great experience it was, I give thanks with them for their assurance of God's justifying or converting grace in their lives. But I also wonder how long ago that event happened and what has been happening since. I find myself wanting to ask, "What is the grace that saved you then doing in your life today, and what do you hope God's grace will do in the future?"

Grace is the love of God that never quits. It is grace that brought us this far, and it is grace that will lead us home.

Your Reflections

- Can you recall times in your life when God's preventing or prevenient grace was at work prior to your response? Describe such a time.

- Were you baptized as a baby or as an adult? Reflect on the meaning of your baptism and record your thoughts or memories.

  Adult
  Rev Boyton was blind but he didn't let that stop him from his calling. He was a great inspiration to me.

> "Grace, the power and the light of God in us, purifying our hearts, transforming us in Christ, making us true [children] of God, enabling us to act in the world as his instruments for the good of all [people] and for his glory."[12]
> —Thomas Merton

> "Salvation begins before we begin and continues long after we thought we were done."[14]
> —William H. Willimon

- How have you experienced God's justifying grace? How would you describe that experience?

  I think God is grace has helped me guide me and keep me on the right path. I have become a better servant since I retired

- Describe some ways in which you have experienced or are experiencing God's sanctifying grace.

  My work with the church programs such as food give away and missions and my work w Habitat

Your Guide to Prayer and Action

O God, how you love me! Your preventing grace began even prior to my conception, drawing me to you even before I could respond. And you didn't stop there! You initiated, enabled, and nurtured me to follow you so that I could grow in love and serve the world. And you didn't stop with me! You promise to restore the whole creation. May I see opportunities today for small acts of love that emerge from your Spirit within me. In Christ's name I pray. Amen.

- Pray through Ephesians 2:1-9 using *Lectio Divina* (refer to the steps on page 119). Use whatever word or phrase God gives you from the Scripture during this time to center your thoughts throughout the day.
- Sit silently for three minutes, reflecting on the ways that God loved you before you could act. Pay attention to your thoughts, feelings, and emotions.

A Disciple's Heart: Daily Workbook

Week 2: Day 4
Baptism: Washed Clean by Grace

Scripture Readings

Read Luke 3:1-3 and Psalm 51:1-10.

Today's Message

Do you ever feel that you need a clean heart? I encourage you to read today's Psalm slowly, attempting to identify with the feelings of the writer.

> *Have mercy on me, God, according to your faithful love!*
> *Wipe away my wrongdoings according to your great compassion!*
> *Wash me completely clean of my guilt;*
> *purify me from my sin!*
>
> *Purify me with hyssop and I will be clean;*
> *wash me and I will be whiter than snow.*
>
> *Hide your face from my sins;*
> *wipe away all my guilty deeds!*
> *Create a clean heart for me, God;*
> *put a new, faithful spirit deep inside me! (Psalm 51:1-2, 7, 9-10)*

When was the last time you felt like that? When have you known that you needed a clean heart?

Tradition says this was the prayer David prayed after his sordid affair with Bathsheba, his deceitful, self-serving murder of her husband, and his fumbling attempt at a political cover-up. The story in 2 Samuel 11:1–12:15 reads like something from a supermarket tabloid. By the time you get through the story, there's no question as to why David needed to pray for a clean heart.

A clean heart was what John the Baptist was offering when he showed up along the Jordan River "calling for people to be baptized to show that they were changing their hearts and lives and wanted God to forgive their sins" (Luke 3:3). The biblical word for that change of heart is *repentance*. It literally means turning away from the old ways of living so that we can live into the kingdom of God revealed in Jesus Christ. It means saying no to our sin so that we can say yes to Christ.

In the Wesleyan tradition, baptism is seen as a "means of grace" by which the Spirit of God is at work to give us a clean heart.

General Sam Houston, the man for whom the city of Houston is named, had lived a rough and tumble life before he was baptized at age sixty-one in the Little Rocky Creek just south of College Station on November 19, 1854. When he was told that his sins had been washed away, Houston is reported to have proclaimed, "I pity the fish downstream."[15]

Houston actually got it right with this humorous remark. We all have old sins, old habits, old attitudes, old hurts, old prejudices, old ways of thinking and living that need to be washed away if we are to find the life God intends for us. We all need a clean heart.

Every time we celebrate the sacrament of baptism in worship, I look forward to the moment when we say to the congregation, "Remember your baptism and be thankful." We are not merely calling people to remember an event in the past. We are inviting them to remember who they are as disciples of Jesus Christ who have been marked by the sign of God's grace in baptism. We are urging them to remember that their baptism is the continuing gift of God's forgiveness and love that is always available to wash away our sin again and again.

We indicate that ongoing work of grace when we pray together:

> Pour out your Holy Spirit,
> to bless this gift of water and those who receive it,
> to wash away their sin
>   and clothe them in righteousness
>   throughout their lives,
> that, dying and being raised with Christ,
>   they may share in his final victory.[17]

Don't miss the continuous present tense in the verbs *wash* and *clothe*. They describe the ongoing work of God's grace throughout our lives.

My partner in this project, Justin LaRosa, shares this witness of God's work of grace in his life:

> Two years after getting sober, I had a deep sense of discontent from the wreckage I had created from my active addiction. I was weighed down by my own sins and by hurts that I was carrying from family-of-origin issues. I began to explore who Christ was and to attend a church regularly—the first time since the age of ten. While I had been baptized as an infant, I felt a deep sense of separateness and the need to be "washed." I continued to be involved in church, and at the pastor's invitation I shared my testimony during the worship service, telling about all the pain, my mistakes, and the way I now could see that God had been with me throughout my active addiction and early life. When I was giving my testimony, I experienced being washed and held by Christ's love. It was as though I "emerged" from the experience clothed in righteousness, leaving the death rags in which I had been wrapped. Afterward I wept the whole way home and throughout the afternoon. I now could see more clearly, and I began living closer to Christ.

Remembering and sharing God's ongoing work of grace in our lives is an important part of our journey of discipleship. Remembering our own baptisms can be an effective way to assist in this reflection. In our own church, we provide an opportunity in worship at the beginning of each year for the congregation to come to the baptismal font one by one, touch the water, and make the sign of the cross on their foreheads. Every year people come to the water—some with tears in their eyes—as they again experience this tangible sign of the intangible grace of God that washes away our sin and gives us a clean heart.

You may or may not have been baptized and you may or may not remember it. The good news is that wherever you are in your faith journey, the grace of God—which the baptismal waters represent—is always available to wash us clean.

Your Reflections

- Name a time in your life when you felt the need to be washed and you prayed for a clean heart.

  when I retired, I had been going to church but not involved so I prayed and got involved in Alex First Christian

- What helps you to recognize the gravity of your sin?

  My bible reading & men's group

- Are there places in your life today where you need a fresh cleansing of God's grace?

  I still need to get out of my comfort zone and be more active

- How have you experienced the continual grace that baptism represents?

  My wife, children and friends are blessings that remind me of God's blessing & grace

Your Guide to Prayer and Action

Recreate me, God of grace and light, day by day and hour by hour. Continue to use the wounds that have been inflicted upon me and those that I have self-created to show that I need you and to draw me nearer to you. I acknowledge in this time and place that it is your love that pieces back together the divine image in me. Wash me, clothe me, and inspire me to live your love today. Amen.

- Pray through Luke 3:1-3 or Psalm 51:1-10 using *Lectio Divina* (refer to the steps on page 119). Use whatever word or phrase God gives you from the Scripture during this time to center your thoughts throughout the day.
- Look back across your faith journey and locate times when you have experienced God's grace in specific ways. Allow those memories to lead you into a prayer of thanks to God.

A Disciple's Heart: Daily Workbook

Week 2: Day 5
Means of Grace: The Table of our Lord

Scripture Reading

Read Luke 24:13-35.

Today's Message

Is there any social event more unpleasant or boring than a pretentious dinner party? It's the kind of dinner where all the guests are on guard like porcupines, trying too hard to be socially correct while attempting—usually with little success—to impress one another with their own importance.

On the other hand, is there anything more enjoyable than a long evening around the dinner table with intimate friends? It's the kind of dinner where there is genuine conversation and honest laughter with no pretense or affectation. It's a feast for glad hearts, a meal shared with unaffected joy.

In our Scripture today, we join two followers of Jesus who were hiking down the road to Emmaus on Sunday afternoon after the crucifixion. One of the most poignant moments in Scripture is when they say, "We had hoped that he was the one who would redeem Israel" (Luke 24:21). They had hoped that Jesus was the one who could save them, but it was all over now. It has all the feeling of a defeated election campaign or the loss of a career. They were so overwhelmed by their despair and sorrow that they didn't recognize the risen Christ when he came and walked along with them. He went with them all the way to Emmaus, listening to their story, reminding them of Scripture and entering into their sadness.

When they reached Emmaus, they invited him to stay for dinner. Luke records that "at the table with them, he took the bread, blessed and broke it, and gave it to them." That's when "their eyes were opened and they recognized him" (24:30-31). They were so excited that they ran all the way back to Jerusalem to tell the other disciples about the way they had experienced the presence of the risen Christ in the breaking of the bread.

Now, that's what I call a memorable dinner party! It might be what Luke had in mind when he wrote that the early Christians broke bread together "with glad and generous hearts" (Acts 2:46 NRSV). That's what we are invited to experience when we break the bread and share the cup in Holy Communion. And that's why John Wesley encouraged the people called Methodists to receive Communion as often as they could.

The expression of Methodism in which I grew up tended to emphasize a penitential attitude toward Communion, as if the primary purpose of the sacrament were to make us feel sorry for our sin. The liturgy focused on our sin and need for God's forgiveness. We came to the table after the Prayer of Humble Access in which we said, "We are not worthy so much as to gather up the crumbs under thy Table."[18]

It's a powerful prayer, every word of which is true. There are times when I need to be humbled by a fresh awareness of my sin and of God's grace. But we tended to be so focused on the penitential aspect of Communion that we seemed to miss out on the joyful part of it.

The dinner party in Emmaus reminds us that the primary focus of the sacrament is not our sin but God's grace. It is not so much a time of mourning because of how bad we are as it is a time of giving thanks for how good God is. On this side of the Resurrection, Communion is not only a time for remembering the darkness of Good Friday; it's also a time to renew our experience of the joy of Easter.

Jesus, whose body was broken and whose blood was shed for us on the cross, is the risen Christ who is alive and walks the road with us. We, like these first disciples, can come from the table saying, "Weren't our hearts on fire . . . ?" (Luke 24:32). That's more than enough reason to celebrate with joy. It was, after all, at the last supper that Jesus said, "Be of good cheer; I have overcome the world" (John 16:33 KJV).

When we break the bread and share the cup, we share the gifts of the extravagantly loving, self-giving God who welcomes us around the dinner table like a generous host, preparing a sumptuous banquet and then sending his servants out into the city streets inviting everyone they can find to get in on the party (see Luke 14:15-24).

Charles Wesley never got over his awe-stricken amazement at the grace of God that we experience in Holy Communion. Look how he celebrates the inexplicable mystery at the heart of the sacrament in the words of this hymn:

> O the depth of love divine, the unfathomable grace!
> Who shall say how bread and wine God into us conveys!
> How the bread His flesh imparts, how the wine transmits His blood,
> Fills His faithful people's hearts with all the life of God![20]

As we've seen, Luke said that one of the things that drew others into the early church was the way they shared their meals "with glad and generous hearts" (Acts 2:46 NRSV). Is there something about the way we share the bread and cup that would attract the attention of others so that they would want to get in on the dinner party too? The promise is that the risen Christ is waiting to celebrate new life with you around his dinner table.

A Disciple's Heart: Daily Workbook

Your Reflections

- Remember your most enjoyable dinner party and your least enjoyable dinner party. Who was there? What made it pleasurable/unpleasant?

- Do you remember the first time you received Communion? If so, what was the experience like? *After I was baptized. Powerful*

- Describe the most powerful experience you have had receiving Communion.

- How often do you receive Communion? Is receiving Communion an important part of your spiritual walk? Do you look forward to it? Why or why not? *Every week. It is important because it reminds me of Gods forgiveness this grace given to us*

A Guide to Prayer and Action

Spirit of the living God, may I open myself to your real Presence today. May I experience that Presence that is always readily available when I center myself in the now—in the present. Orient my thoughts and attention to each moment today. In Christ's name. Amen.

- Follow the instructions on page 120 for a time of centering prayer. Read aloud Luke 24:13-35 to begin your prayer period, or use another passage of your own choosing.
- Contact a friend or fellow sojourner to discuss the meaning and significance of the Eucharist, Holy Communion. Share your answer to the last question above.

Week 3
By the Power of the Spirit

None of the advancements in medical science in my lifetime is more amazing than heart transplants. When the biblical writers spoke of the heart as the central core of human life, they never could have conceived of the possibility that one day we would actually be able to replace a broken, diseased heart with a healthy, life-giving one.

John Wesley never could have imagined medical heart transplants, but he knew that God is in the spiritual heart transplant business. After his heart-warming experience at Aldersgate, Wesley became an evangelist for receiving a new heart as a gift of grace from the God whose only Son gave his life to make this exchange possible. He knew that God could take a heart of stone and transform it into a heart of flesh (see Ezekiel 36:26).

For disciples in the Wesleyan tradition, the heart of the matter is always a matter of the heart—a heart transformed by the love of God into the likeness of Jesus Christ. It is the fulfillment of the promise God made to Jeremiah: "I will give them a heart to know me, for I am the Lord. They will be my people, and I will be their God, for they will return to me with all their heart" (Jeremiah 24:7).

God's work of spiritual cardiology happens in our lives through the presence and work of the Holy Spirit.

- It is by the Spirit that we become aware of our need for a new heart, are drawn to Christ, experience God's grace, and enter into the life of discipleship.
- It is through the Spirit that God's love takes up residence within us and begins perfecting us into the likeness of Christ.
- It is in the power of the Spirit that we are sent into the world to be the agents of God's transformation in this world.
- And it will be by the Spirit that God's salvation ultimately will be accomplished in the whole creation.

This week we will discover the Holy Spirit as the "divine cardiologist" who is constantly at work to take out of us a heart of stone and give us a heart of flesh—a heart throbbing with the love of God in Jesus Christ. May we hear the Holy Spirit pleading with us to accept God's gift of a new heart.

WEEK 3: DAY 1
SHALL WE DANCE?

Scripture Reading
Read John 14:1-21.

Today's Message
The disciples were absolutely baffled by what Jesus was saying. We would be too. They were confused by the way Jesus talked about himself, about God, and about the Holy Spirit as they shared what would be their last Passover meal together:

> *"I am in the Father and the Father is in me." (John 14:10)*

> *"I will ask the Father and he will send another Companion who will be with you forever. This Companion is the Spirit of Truth, whom the world can't receive because it neither sees him nor recognizes him. You know him, because he lives with you and will be with you." (John 14:16-17)*

> *"I am in my Father, you are in me, and I am in you." (John 14:20)*

> *"The Holy Spirit, whom the Father will send in my name will teach you everything and will remind you of everything I told you." (John 14:26)*

What kind of talk is this? Jesus refers to himself as the Son. He talks about God as his Father. He promises the Holy Spirit as our Companion, Advocate, or Comforter (depending on the translation). It took the early Christians three hundred years to label this understanding of God as the *Trinity*. But it can still be just as baffling to us as it was to the disciples.

How do we get our heads around the Trinity? Better yet, how do we get in on the action of the Trinity? What if the Trinity is not so much a theoretical proposition to be explained as it is a living reality to be experienced?

I used to say that the Trinity is like water. It is always H_2O—two parts hydrogen and one part oxygen—but it can be experienced in three ways as liquid, solid, or gas. The problem is that there is nothing personal about that comparison, and everything Jesus said about the Spirit is extravagantly relational.

So, I changed my analogy. I then said that I am Jim Harnish. That's who I've always been; it's who I will always be. But to my mother, I am a son; to my wife, I am a husband; to my daughters, I am a father. I am one person in three relationships. That worked until I became a grandfather, because I couldn't add a fourth person to the Trinity!

Then I discovered the *Untermyer Fountain* in New York City's Central Park. The original bronze, *Three Dancing Maidens*, was made in Germany by artist Walter Schott in 1910; this cast of the original was placed in Central Park in 1947. (You can find a picture of the fountain on the Internet.) The sculptor created three women holding hands and dancing in a circle with such fluid movement that they appear to be in perpetual motion. Each figure is distinct, but they are inseparably bound together in a dance that overflows with life and joy.

I began to imagine the Trinity as a glorious dance in which the Father, Son, and Holy Spirit are in perfect harmony—each unique; each complimenting the other; all of them in joy-filled, love-soaked, life-giving, never-ending movement together.

Jesus' words to the disciples in John 14 are not intended to explain the Trinity but to invite us to join in the dance of life and love that is shared by the Father, Son, and Holy Spirit. Don't miss the way Jesus used the word "in."

"I am *in* the Father and the Father is *in* me" (v. 10, emphasis added).

"You will know that I am *in* my Father, and you *in* me, and I *in* you" (v. 20 NRSV, emphasis added).

Charles Wesley described the way we enter into the dance of the Trinity in his hymn "Maker in Whom We Live." He said that we experience God as the Creator "in whom we live, we are and move"; we experience the Son as "the Incarnate Deity" through whom we know God's saving grace; and we experience the Holy Spirit as the "sacred energy" of God's "heart-renewing power."[2]

We are invited to join in the dance with the Father, Son, and Holy Spirit. But we must remember that learning to dance takes time and practice. We have to learn the steps, feel the rhythm, and learn to do it together in order to experience the beauty of the dance. We may be awkward at first, but the spiritual disciplines we are exploring in this study are patient instructors as we step onto the dance floor and join the dance.

The question is not whether we can explain the Trinity but whether we are experiencing the reality of it. Shall we dance?

Your Reflections

- How do you understand the Trinity? How would you describe the Trinity to a person who knows nothing about it? *I still like the water analogy*

- How have you experienced God as Father? Creator?

  I see God as my Holy Father and protector

- How have you experienced God as Son? Redeemer?

  I see Jesus as my guide & savior

- How have you experienced God as Spirit? Companion?

  I see the Holy Spirit as my guide & conscience

Your Guide to Prayer and Action

God, may I respond today to your invitation to dance. May I strive to remember you in every rhythm of my life. Whether I am in a time of joy, frustration, waiting, hoping, or fear, I offer myself to you and pray that I may see your invitation into deeper fellowship. Amen.

- Pray through John 14:1-21 using *Lectio Divina* (refer to the steps on page 119). Whatever word or phrase God gives you from the Scripture during this time, use it all throughout the day to center your thoughts.
- Reflect on this question: How would you describe each person in the Trinity?

WEEK 3: DAY 2
WHEN THE SPIRIT COMES

Scripture Reading

Read Acts 1:1-11.

Today's Message

It was forty days after Easter; forty days since the women found the empty tomb; forty days since the shocking, unexpected announcement: "He is not here; he has risen!" (Matthew 28:6 NIV).

For faithful readers of the Bible, the mention of forty days conjures up a flood of memories from the history of God's relationship with the Hebrew people: the forty days Noah spent in the ark, the forty years the children of Israel wandered in the wilderness, the forty days Moses was on Mount Sinai receiving the Ten Commandments, the forty days the prophet Elijah spent on Mount Horeb where he experienced the "still, small voice" of God (1 Kings 19:12 KJV), and the forty days that Jesus spent in the wilderness wrestling with temptation before the start of his ministry.

We quickly get the point that for the biblical writers, "forty days" represents the time it takes to prepare God's people for a new experience of God's presence and a new sense of calling to God's mission in the world.

The biblical pattern suggests that we are not ready to do God's work in the world until we experience God's work in our hearts. It's enough to make us wary of quick fixes, overnight sensations, or instant spiritual maturity. It's the invitation for every disciple to nurture the disciplines of silence, prayer, and Scripture meditation by which the Spirit can prepare us to be effective witnesses for Jesus Christ. This also may be the most important lesson we can learn from the early Methodists at Oxford—the life-sustaining necessity of spiritual preparation for active ministry.

During the forty days after Jesus' resurrection, Jesus kept showing up where the disciples least expected to find him: walking along the Emmaus Road, revealing his scars in the upper room, fixing breakfast on the beach for the fishermen. Along the way, he kept promising something that was yet to come: "You will receive power when the Holy Spirit has come upon you, and you will be my witnesses in Jerusalem, in all Judea and Samaria, and to the end of the earth" (Acts 1:8).

Then he was gone. Luke records, "He was lifted up and a cloud took him out of their sight" (Acts 1:9).

I can't explain the astrophysics of the Ascension. The details of how it happened are not as important as what it means: Jesus Christ has been lifted up above every other authority, ruler, or power. It is a visual affirmation of the promise that one day "everyone in heaven, on earth, and under the earth might bow and every tongue confess that Jesus Christ is Lord" (Philippians 2:10-11).

If anyone ever knew what it meant to be powerless, it had to be those fearful, inadequate, absolutely powerless disciples. As they waited, watched, and prayed in Jerusalem, all they had was a memory and a promise.

A Disciple's Heart: Daily Workbook

Jesus told the disciples to remember what they had heard him say about the Holy Spirit (see Acts 1:4-5). Across those forty days, the disciples must have repeated over and over again what Jesus had said at the Last Supper when he referred to the Holy Spirit as *paraclete* (John 14:16). The Greek root word is *paraklétos*, which means "called to one's aid."[3] In the legal system, it referred to an advocate who came to represent another in court. This word captures all of the imagery of the English translations of Comforter, Companion, and Advocate. If the disciples were going to be witnesses to Christ in this world, they would need the Spirit in all of those ways.

The disciples also had heard Jesus' promise that the Spirit would come to represent, indeed to re-present, himself in their lives. They would not be on their own. The Spirit would be with them and within them to remind them of who Jesus was, what Jesus said, and how Jesus lived. Everything the Spirit would do in and through them would be consistent with what they had experienced with Jesus.

I find great assurance in remembering what the disciples had heard from Jesus. In different ways and at different times, I need to know the Spirit as Comforter, Companion, or Advocate. I also find reassurance in knowing that the work of the Spirit is consistent with the words and way of Jesus. The first questions I ask when I hear people talk about the Holy Spirit are these: Does it look like Jesus? Is this something Jesus would be doing?

Along with all they remembered, Jesus also gave the disciples the promise of power to be his witnesses in this world. This is not power as the world defines power. It is not self-serving, autocratic, or top-down power. It is the power to be the agents of God's love, healing, reconciliation, and peace in a broken world infected with violence, conflict, and pain. It is the power we need to live the way Jesus lived, love the way Jesus loved, teach what Jesus taught, heal the way Jesus healed, die the way Jesus died, and rise to new life the way God raised Jesus from the dead. The power of the Holy Spirit comes to enable us to be a part of God's new creation, God's re-creation of this world.

This power is still available to us today. Through the power of the Holy Spirit within us, we can be Jesus' witnesses in our world.

> "We need to follow the Holy Spirit into our own desert. It is that place of testing where we can face and be freed from our many falsehoods and facades and where we can begin to find our true security in God. . . . It is that place of renewal and refreshment where the angels come to strengthen us for whatever tasks and trials lie ahead."[4]
> —Trevor Hudson

Your Reflections

- When have you experienced a time that God was preparing you for a new experience of God's presence or a new sense of calling to be on mission in the world?

when I went on mission trips to Mississippi

- Write about a time when you have experienced God's work in your heart. What about it was painful? Joyful? Confusing?

  when I went out to look for home for our Reach work camp it was painful to see the poverty we have right here. I know we helped a lot of people but it was only a drop.

- Describe a time when the Holy Spirit enabled you to be a witness for Christ—whether it was in word or in deed.

  when I delivered food to the needy in Alex.

- Describe a time when you experienced the Holy Spirit as Comforter, Companion, Helper, or Advocate.

  The Holy Spirit has helped me get through my depression at learning I have coliac desease

Your Guide to Prayer and Action

O Holy Spirit of God, come to my aid! Come alongside me. Take up residence within me. Make me aware of your presence and empower me to be a witness in the world of your love, power, and reconciliation. Amen.

- Practice the Saint Ignatius prayer method following the instructions on page 121. Use Acts 1:4-11, one of the narrative Scriptures listed on page 121, or a narrative passage of your own choosing.
- Spend a few minutes thinking about how you can be a witness in the world this week. Is there some person, circumstance, or situation that you can bring love to in a small act of compassion?

Week 3: Day 3
This Gift Is for You!

Scripture Readings

Read Acts 2:1-21 and 1 Corinthians 12:1-27.

Today's Message

The disciples never got over what happened on the day of Pentecost. If we had been there, we would have had a hard time getting over it too!

In trying to describe something that was indescribable, the best Luke could say was that it was "like the howling of a fierce wind"; he wrote that Jesus' followers saw "what seemed to be individual flames of fire alighting on each one of them" (Acts 2:2-3). No one could fully explain it, and no one would get over it. All they could say was that they were filled with the Holy Spirit.

These ordinary, uneducated disciples were given the ability to tell the story of Jesus so that everyone could understand it in their own native language.

Luke reports that everyone was amazed and perplexed. They wondered what in God's name—literally, in God's name—was going on. And then, perhaps most amazing of all, Peter—the guy who just a few weeks ago had denied that he had ever known Jesus—stood up in front of the crowd to explain what was happening. He quoted the Old Testament prophet Joel:

> In the last days, God says,
> I will pour out my Spirit on all people.
>> Your sons and daughters will prophesy.
>> Your young will see visions.
>> Your elders will dream dreams.
>> Even upon my servants, men and women,
>>> I will pour out my Spirit in those days,
>>> and they will prophesy. . . .
> And everyone who calls on the name of the Lord will be saved. (Acts 2:17-21)

Luke writes that three thousand people were baptized that day. It was a day they would never forget.

One of the reasons we do not read about the disciples discussing or reviewing what happened on Pentecost is that it kept happening. The presence and power of the Holy Spirit was not just the memory of a monumental moment in the past but a continuing reality in the present that equipped them for ministry in the future. It became the way they lived.

The Pentecostal pyrotechnics quieted down. The "howling of a fierce wind" became more like a steady blowing breeze. The flames that danced around the room became a fire in their bones, a burning passion to share the good news of God's love in Christ with anyone and everyone who had not experienced it.

The ability to tell the story of Jesus so that people could hear it in their own native language became the courage to use the one language they knew to communicate the gospel so that all people—in their own culture, language, and ethnic tradition—could claim it for their own.

The pyrotechnics may have faded away, but the fire never went out. The presence of the Holy Spirit became the power that transformed their lives—a power that continues to transform the life of the church today.

The Apostle Paul wasn't there on Pentecost. He didn't feel the wind or see the flames. But in his letters he describes what he calls "gifts" that the Spirit gives to every follower of Jesus Christ:

> *There are different spiritual gifts but the same Spirit; and there are different ministries and the same Lord; and there are different activities but the same God who produces all of them in everyone. A demonstration of the Spirit is given to each person for the common good. (1 Corinthians 12:4-7)*

The gifts of the Spirit are not given to make us tingle all over or to make us more "spiritual" than others. The gifts of the Holy Spirit are given "for the common good." They are given to enable us to serve as Jesus served, to love as Jesus loved, to care as Jesus cared, and to give ourselves to others the way Jesus gave himself to us.

That's usually the way the Spirit moves today—not with rushing wind and tongues of fire. Not with explosive shaking of houses or miraculous speaking in other languages. Instead, the Spirit of God continues to be at work to accomplish God's saving purpose in this world through ordinary people who are given extraordinary gifts for the purpose of sharing God's love in tangible ways. Though the gifts are different, all are given by the same Spirit for the common good.

A friend was disappointed when a spiritual gifts assessment revealed that his primary gift is administration. He had hoped for what he considered a more interesting gift. He was disappointed when two other gift assessment tools turned up the same results. Then he led one of our mission teams to South Africa. The others members of the team had what he thought were more important gifts of apostleship, exhortation, and healing. But during the preparation and throughout the journey, he discovered that without his gift of administration, the entire team would have been confused and ineffective. His gift enabled others to use their gifts in ways that fulfilled God's calling in their lives. He was gifted by the Spirit for the common good.

The disciples never got over what happened on Pentecost. Have we?

Your Reflections

- Write about a time when you have been "amazed and perplexed" because of what God was doing in your life or someone else's.

  I am amazed at how Bob Doery serve on Missions & perplexed that I hesitate to do more

- How has Pentecost happened in your own life? Describe it here.

- What spiritual gift do you have that God can use for the common good? (If you are not aware of your spiritual gifts, take an online spiritual gifts assessment as directed in Your Guide to Prayer and Action.)

  I serve through Habitat, and the Lions

- Describe the ways in which your gifts have been confirmed in community. If they have not been confirmed, pray about the ways in which you can live out God's call to use your gifts.

  Many people have come to me for help with glasses

Your Guide to Prayer and Action

Spirit of the living God, give me passion for the common good. May I live today with the knowledge that your presence and power are within me. Show me opportunites to share the gifts you have given me to bring forth your love. Amen.

- Practice the Saint Ignatius prayer method following the instructions on page 121. Use Acts 2:1-21, one of the narrative Scriptures listed on page 121, or a narrative passage of your own choosing.
- If you have not had your spiritual gift confirmed in community, take an online spiritual gifts assessment such as the one found at ministrymatters.com/spiritualgifts (first sign up or sign in, and then you will be able to take the quiz). Talk to your pastor or small group after receiving the results.

> God doesn't give people the Holy Spirit in order to let them enjoy the spiritual equivalent of a day at Disneyland. . . . The point of the Spirit is to enable those who follow Jesus to take into all the world the news that he is Lord, that he has won the victory over the forces of evil, that a new world has opened up, and that we are to help make it happen.[5]
> —N. T. Wright

WEEK 3: DAY 4
SANCTIFICATION IN THE REFINER'S FIRE

Scripture Reading
Read Malachi 3:1-4.

Today's Message
My grandchildren love to build a fire in our fireplace, even in the heat of the Florida summer. They're fascinated with it. As a responsible grandparent and a one-time Boy Scout, it's my job to warn them that if they get too close to the fire, they will get burned—and they might burn the house down in the process!

That's essentially what Malachi was doing in our Scripture for today: warning the people not to get burned. You see, five centuries before Christ, he predicted that the Lord would come to take up residence among them. That was very good news. That's why they had rebuilt the Temple. They wanted the Almighty God to be present and alive among them, just as we long for God's presence to be a living reality in our experience. But then Malachi asked these disturbing questions: "Who can endure the day of his coming, and who can stand when he appears?" (Malachi 3:2 NRSV).

The writer of Psalm 24:3-4 asked the same questions: "Who shall ascend the hill of the Lord? / And who shall stand in his holy place?" The answer came back: "Those who have clean hands and pure hearts, / who do not lift up their souls to what is false" (NRSV).

Clean hands. Pure hearts. That's almost as high as the standard Jesus set when he said that we are to be perfect—complete, whole—in our love even as our Father in heaven is perfect in his love (Matthew 5:48). No wonder Malachi said, "He *is* like a refiner's fire" (3:2 NKJV). Get close to the presence of God and there is a good chance that you will get burned.

There was a time when many people began the journey of faith because they were afraid of the fires of hell. A fire-breathing preacher such as Jonathan Edwards would dangle them over the flames of hell through impassioned preaching, and they would come running to the altar.

Times have changed. Fear of hellfire isn't what it used to be. Fear is not the place where most people begin their discipleship journey. People are more likely to be drawn to Jesus on the basis of his love, grace, and goodness than on the basis of their fear of eternal damnation. But that doesn't mean that the refiner's fire has been extinguished. The journey toward perfection always leads through the fire. Not the fires of an eternal hell, but the fire of God's refining love. Not flames on the other side of death, but the purifying flames of God's grace in the present. Not a fire in some distant Hades, but the fire of the Spirit that ignites a fiery passion in our hearts.

The same Spirit that caused Wesley to say that his heart was "strangely warmed" at Aldersgate is the Spirit who comes as the refiner's fire to burn away the dross that keeps us from the life of holiness we deeply desire.

A Disciple's Heart: Daily Workbook

Dross is defined as "unwanted material that is removed from a mineral (such as gold) to make it better."[6] It is the word Charles Wesley used when he wrote these words:

> O that in me the sacred fire
> Might now begin to glow;
> Burn up the dross of base desire
> And make the mountains flow!
>
> Refining fire, go through my heart,
> Illuminate my soul;
> Scatter thy life through every part
> And sanctify the whole.[7]

Sanctification is the theological word we use to name the refining process by which the Spirit of God purifies our intentions, purges our hearts of anything that gets in the way of God's highest and best will for us, and prepares us to offer ourselves as the agents of God's love.

Don't miss the purpose of the refining fire: "That they may offer to the LORD /An offering in righteousness" (Malachi 3:3 NKJV). The refining fire of the Spirit prepares us to offer our lives as the gift of God's love to the world.

Sometimes the refining fire goes through our hearts in deeply personal ways as we wrestle with the often subtle imperfections and impurities in our lives. In the sixteenth century, Saint John of the Cross called this the dark night of the soul.

Sometimes the refining fire purifies us through the accountabily of other disciples—through people who love us enough to tell us the truth we may not want to hear. People who love us enough to help us see the dross that gets in the way of God's work in our lives. That was the purpose of the Holy Club begun by John Wesley and his companions at Oxford.

Sometimes the refining fire does its work as we face the changing circumstances of life—events that test our integrity, push up against our deepest values, and challenge our most deeply held assumptions.

So, what will it look like for the refining fire to go through your heart? No one can answer that question for you. All I can say with certainty is that along the way to perfection, each of us will go through the fire not once but many times as the Spirit uncovers the dross of bitter attitudes, corrupted values, buried hurts, nagging habits, and plain old selfishness. And the promise is that when we go through the fire, we will discover—as Shadrach, Meshach, and Abednego did—that there is one in the fire with us who "is like the Son of God" (Daniel 3:25 NKJV).

Your Reflections

- Did you initially respond to Christ's invitation because of love or because of fear?

Love

- Describe the way in which initially responding from love or from fear has shaped your journey with Christ and the church as well as your understanding of God.

  I was blessed by a loving family & Sunday school teachers who guided me with a love of God & his people

- How is God refining you? What dross (unwanted material) do you have that is blocking you from God?

  I have too many distractions, worries & desires that get in my path & these readings & discussions are helping me refocus on God's path

- The first step to change is always recognition. Name the ways you have come to recognize that your dross is preventing you from living the life you have been called to live.

  I know what the distraction are and now it is matter of focasing on the positive path God sets for us & letting the Holy Spirit guide me

Your Guide to Prayer and Action

Make in me a clean heart, God. Instill not only an acute awareness of the dross in my life but also a willingness to change. May I surrender to the refining fire of your love. Amen.

- Pray through Malachi 3:1-4 using *Lectio Divina* (refer to the steps on page 119). Whatever word or phrase God gives you from the Scripture during this time, use it throughout the day to center your thoughts.
- Reflect on the ways that you can surrender your "dross" to Christ.
- Reach out to a person or persons with whom you can be accountable. Share with them the dross in your life.

A Disciple's Heart: Daily Workbook

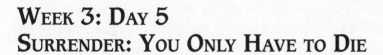

WEEK 3: DAY 5
SURRENDER: YOU ONLY HAVE TO DIE

Scripture Reading

Read Luke 19:28-44.

Today's Message

One of the best ways to read the Bible is to ask: Where do I find myself in this story? With which character do I feel the closest connection? Sometimes the answer will surprise us.

I was preparing for Palm Sunday, living into the story of Jesus' entry into Jerusalem, when I found myself identifying with the unnamed owners of the donkey that Jesus rode into the city. When they saw the disciples untying the colt, they asked, "What are you doing? Where do you think you're going with our colt?" (Luke 19:33, author paraphrase).

I could understand their reaction. After all, if I saw a couple of strangers taking my car, my response would be very similar.

The only answer the donkey owners received was that the Master needed it. But that was enough. The owners let go of their donkey and allowed Jesus to use it.

The story raises all sorts of intriguing questions that the Gospel writers aren't the least bit interested in answering. Who were these donkey owners? Were they in the Rent-A-Donkey business? Had Jesus paid for an advance reservation with his Visa card? What happened to the donkey after the parade?

As I lived into the story, I realized that the Gospel writers weren't interested in those questions because none of them gets close to the deeper, more disturbing questions the story began to raise in my soul:

- What if it were *my* donkey?
- Would I be willing to let it go?
- What if, like the owners of that donkey, I am being called to give up something of myself to Jesus?
- What if the way toward perfection is the way of surrender, the way of letting go?

Those questions led me to some of the most challenging words Jesus spoke:

> *"All who want to come after me must say no to themselves, take up their cross daily, and follow me. All who want to save their lives will lose them. But all who lose their lives because of me will save them." (Luke 9:23-24)*

> *"Unless a grain of wheat falls into the earth and dies, it can only be a single seed. But if it dies, it bears much fruit." (John 12:24)*

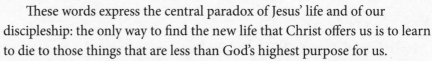

> You are never so much your own than when you are most His.[9]
> —E. Stanley Jones

These words express the central paradox of Jesus' life and of our discipleship: the only way to find the new life that Christ offers us is to learn to die to those things that are less than God's highest purpose for us.

E. Stanley Jones, one of the most outstanding global witnesses for the gospel in the twentieth century, often described one of the central themes of his life as the discovery that we are not called to imitate Jesus but to surrender ourselves to Him. He explained the difference between "self-realization" and "self-surrender," saying that in self-realization we assume the answers to life's questions are inside us, whereas in self-surrender to Christ we find our answers in him. Based on Jesus' promise that it is in losing our life that we find it (Luke 17:33), he taught that we find ourselves when we lose ourselves in "surrender to creative love."[10]

I experience this kind of surrender as the movement from a "me first" mind-set to a "Christ first" mind-set. It is the movement from self-serving to self-giving, from living life my way to living life Christ's way.

There was a time when I was searching for a one-time moment of total surrender that would take care of these issues for the rest of my life. But I have learned along the way that surrender to Christ is not a one-time event but a pattern of living in continuous surrender that allows the love of God in Christ to become a continuing source of transformation in my life. Surrender is the way I participate in the process of being made perfect in love.

The transforming paradox of the gospel is that new life comes only through death. The journey toward perfection always leads to the cross—where we die to old attitudes, habits, assumptions, sins, and ways of thinking and living so that we can be raised to the new life that Christ has for us. It's what the Apostle Paul meant when he wrote, "I have been crucified with Christ and I no longer live, but Christ lives in me. And the life that I now live in my body, I live by faith, indeed, by the faithfulness of God's Son, who loved me and gave himself for me" (Galatians 2:20).

As I discovered in my preparation for Palm Sunday, the question we should ask is not "Who were the donkey owners?" The truth is that, in a sense, we all are donkey owners. The important question is "Will we surrender to Jesus—all that we have and all that we are?" If we will surrender, God's saving love can become a tangible reality in this world through us.

Your Reflections

- With whom do you most identify in today's Scripture?

  The 2 disciples

- What have you been called to surrender to Jesus in the past?

  My time for playing golf or relaxing

- Are you being called now to give up something of yourself to Jesus? What is your current "donkey"?

  fear of failure

Your Guide to Prayer and Action

"Take, Lord, and receive all my liberty, my memory, my understanding, and my entire will—all that I have and call my own. You have given it all to me. Lord, I return it. Everything is yours; do with it what you will. Give me only your love and grace. This is enough for me."[11]

—Reuben Job

- Practice the Saint Ignatius prayer method following the instructions on page 121. Use Luke 19:28-44, one of the narrative Scriptures listed on page 121, or a narrative passage of your own choosing.
- Reread the words from E. Stanley Jones on the preceding page and listen for the way they may lead you to a new place of surrender to Christ.

WEEK 4
THE COMPANY OF THE COMMITTED

What sustains a follower of Christ along the way toward Christian perfection? What keeps us on the way when other ways seem more appealing? How do we hold on to the vision of the kingdom of God, coming on earth as it is in heaven, when everything on earth seems to be stacked against it?

Stephen Bauman, pastor of Christ Church in New York City, lifted up the example of Dr. Martin Luther King, Jr., who often acknowledged the ways in which the forces of bitterness, hatred, evil, and sin conspired to hold back the way of truth, justice, and peace. He pointed out that Dr. King was sustained along the way by being a part of a company that "was striving for something higher, bigger, brighter and frankly, holier than the cultural values of his day. They were companions committed to a justice born from faith." He concluded that "we are so very much better off in the company of friends who seek the same goal."[1]

The good news for every disciple is that we do not make this journey toward perfection alone. We share our lives with a company of friends, fellow disciples who are drawn into the body of Christ. I like the way Quaker theologian Elton Trueblood described it: "the Company of the Committed."[2]

> "The fellowship of Christian brethren is a gift of grace, a gift of the Kingdom of God. . . . It is grace, nothing but grace, that we are allowed to live in community with Christian brethren."[3]
> —Dietrich Bonhoeffer

Life in the body of Christ is never easy. Sometimes the church feels like a cage full of porcupines. Because of our imperfection, we almost inevitably bump into each other, hurt each other, and are tempted to pull away into our own private corner of individualized spirituality.

No matter how far we've come in the process of being made perfect in love, it is usually in our relationships with other imperfect disciples that we discover just how imperfect we are. At the same time, it is in the company of other disciples that we find support in our weakness, accountability for our discipleship, and the encouragement to keep on striving toward the perfection to which Christ has called us. It is the very human expression of the body of Christ at work in tangible and touchable ways in our world through which the love of God that became a reality in Jesus becomes a reality in the lives of others.

This week we will discover some of the ways in which being a member of "the Company of the Committed" becomes an essential element of our journey toward Christian perfection.

WEEK 4: DAY 1
JOIN THE CLUB

Scripture Reading

Read Luke 6:12-16.

> "The physical presence of other Christians is a source of incomparable joy and strength to the believer. . . . Christianity means community through Jesus Christ and in Jesus Christ."[4]
> —Dietrich Bonhoeffer

Today's Message

It's no small thing that when Jesus set out to begin his ministry, he called twelve men to be his disciples. It's clear that Jesus never intended to do his ministry alone. He formed these very ordinary men into an extraordinary company of friends who would become the apostolic cadre that, by the power of the Holy Spirit, would continue his ministry into the future. Jesus' life with the disciples becomes the model for the way his followers in every age are called to be in community with one another.

In the spring of 1729, John and Charles Wesley and a few other Oxford students were drawn together with a clear and simple desire to live a holy life. When other students observed the orderly way in which they practiced their spiritual disciplines, they sarcastically called them the "Holy Club."

It would be easy to romanticize these groups as if the participants were always in perfect harmony with each other. By contrast, Benjamin Ingham's journal reveals differences between the group members that sometimes resulted in strained relationships. But they were bound together in their shared desire to be fully devoted followers of Jesus Christ. That desire led John Wesley to Aldersgate Street where the Spirit lit a fire of divine love in his heart that ignited a movement that continues to this day. Wherever the Methodist movement has lived up to its heritage, it has thrived through some form of small group community that is modeled after the Holy Club in which disciples become faithful companions in "the Company of the Committed."

As a college student, I became involved with a small group of guys in my dormitory who wanted to experience something of the same spiritual energy that had been at work in the Holy Club. We met weekly for Bible study, prayer, and the sharing of our lives. In our own imperfect way, we made stumbling attempts at holding each other accountable for our spiritual growth.

It didn't last very long. With sophomoric arrogance, we didn't think we needed the kind of spiritual mentor that Benjamin Ingham found in Wesley. But the laughter, friendship, and bumbling attempt at spiritual discipline of those late-night meetings reflected a Wesleyan way of sharing life together.

Years later, one of the guys from that college dorm group joined a clergy covenant group of which we both are still a part. That clergy group has been together more than three decades. We've seen each other through all the joys and pains that life can bring.

Here's the way Justin LaRosa describes his experience of a covenant or accountability group.

Our men's accountability group had been meeting for three years. We focused on holding each other accountable to spiritual practices and praying for one another. We were growing but were staying near the surface. We all sensed we needed to go deeper, so we reformatted our group to share around five things: our spiritual practice commitments for the previous week and the week upcoming, where we saw God at work in our lives, our sins, our prayer requests, and the people we needed to forgive. Each member hit all five areas and then there was opportunity for feedback. One member was struggling with an addiction. He seemed to talk week after week about his slips. The group offered support and suggested accountability through a number of means. He resisted. After a series of weeks, one member strongly suggested that he was not ready to let it go and to let us know when he was ready and we would be willing to support him. It was tough love, but it helped this brother eventually engage his community for support in his quest for deeper love.

The encouragement and accountability that Benjamin Ingham found in the Holy Club, that I experienced in a college dormitory, and that Justin described above are not unique. They are the ongoing gifts of God's grace that enable women and men to continue to grow as disciples of Jesus Christ in a wide variety of small groups, classes, and ministry teams as they share their lives together in "the Company of the Committed."

Your Reflections

- Name one person (other than a significant other or spouse) with whom you can be totally honest about all of your faults, strengths, fears, and hopes.

Ed Headly

- Reflect on a current or past group that served to spiritually develop you. What were the attributes or values expressed in the group that allowed you to grow?

  Our men's Breakfast group have supported each other with prayer & discussion of books we read

- List below an issue for which you need accountability. It can be lack of discipline for spiritual practices, a person whom you haven't forgiven, or an attitude that is blocking you from God or others.

  I need accountability in getting out of my comfort zone and actively seek to witness to non church going friends & acquaints

- Think about your small group (if you have one) or a close spiritual friend. List the ways that you can be a blessing to them/this person this week. *I need to reach out to members of our group and learn if anything is troubling them. I need to work w Jim T to see what service our group can do*

Your Guide to Prayer and Action

God, I pray for my spiritual friends, for those people who make me better and who journey with me. May we lift one another up in times of hardship and celebrate one another in times of abundance. I ask that I not only be honest with you in my prayer time but also with them. Renew the divine image within me and make me an Image-bearer in all that I do today. Amen.

- Pray through Luke 6:12-16 using *Lectio Divina* (refer to the steps on page 119). Whatever word or phrase God gives you from the Scripture during this time, use it throughout the day to center your thoughts.
- In today's reading, we see that Jesus spent the night praying and the next day called his disciples. Spend time in prayer today interceding for those people with whom you are in ministry. If you do not have a version of the Holy Club, pray that God might reveal some people with whom you can make the journey.

WEEK 4: DAY 2
YOU DON'T HAVE TO FACE LIFE ALONE

Scripture Reading

Read 1 Corinthians 12:12-27.

Today's Message

I've had the joy of performing the role of the father of the bride for both of our daughters. We have lots of pictures and videos of both weddings, but no picture can take the place of actually being there.

Our firstborn daughter, who writes a business blog, referred to her sister's wedding as "the end-all-be-all face-to-face meeting." She said that in the world of live streaming and video technology, "there are a million ways to 'be there' without really being there," but the idea of a "virtual wedding" seems downright absurd. She wrote:

> Would it ever be the same if the bride and groom were both on iChat when they said 'I DO'? Instead, they stand face-to-face, hand-in-hand, and promise to love each other in sickness and in health, until death does them part. . . . The pictures and videos won't replace the experience for those of us who watched it happen.[6]

She concluded that social media and virtual technology will never take the place of the relationships that are formed when people interact face-to-face.

That principle is just as true for Christian disciples as it is for weddings and business meetings. No matter how effective our technology may be, there's nothing quite like being with the congregation in worship or sharing the friendship and accountability of a small group. Nothing can take the place of holding another person's hand in a time of grief or hearing someone's laughter in a time of joy. Nothing can take the place of serving the needs of others in partnership with other followers of Christ. Nothing can replace the face-to-face meeting of disciples in the body of Christ.

Our reading for today comes from Paul's letter to the most contentious, conflicted, and messed up congregation he had to deal with. My guess is that some of the folks in Corinth were surprised to hear him say, "Christ is just like the human body—a body is a unit and has many parts; and all the parts of the body are one body, even though there are many" (1 Corinthians 12:12).

A few verses later he resorts to what my college debate coach would have called *reductio ad absurdam*. It's as absurd as a virtual wedding for the foot to say, "I'm not part of the body because I'm not a hand" (1 Corinthians 12:15). It reduces the argument to absurdity because it is so obvious that every part of the human body is connected to every other part. If you've ever broken your toe, you know that a sore toe affects your whole body.

Paul drives his point home with these words: "If one part suffers, all the parts suffer with it; if one part gets the glory, all the parts celebrate with it. You are the body of Christ and parts of each other" (1 Corinthians 12:26-27).

According to the New Testament, there is no such thing as private, individual Christianity. John Wesley taught that "Christianity is essentially a social religion; and that to turn it into a solitary religion, is to destroy it."[7] This means that no follower of Jesus needs to go through life alone.

Within every congregation you can find people who would say that they found the power to make it through difficult times because of the strength they received from other people in their congregation. Others would say that their joy was multiplied exponentially because they shared it with their fellow disciples. Many would say that their spiritual growth has been in direct proportion to their engagement with other disciples.

Justin described the way that being a part of community made a difference for his family after a break-in at their home:

> I received a panicked call from my wife in the middle of the day saying that someone was breaking into our home. The culprits rang the doorbell and when no one answered, they began kicking in the door. They ran away when they stepped inside and saw my wife talking to the 911 operator. Deeply shaken, she received many expressions of support through social media, but the thing that made the biggest difference in the days ahead was the personal care she received from the people with whom she shared her experience and processed her fear. Face-to-face presence brought us through the crisis.

Here's where Paul's analogy breaks down: hands and feet have no choice about being connected in the human body. But in the body of Christ, we get to choose. We can choose to connect with the rest of the body or to live in isolation. We can choose the degree to which we will enter into Christian community and the degree to which we will try to make it on our own. I've seen it happen both ways.

> Partakers of the Savior's grace,
> The same in mind and heart,
> Nor joy, nor grief, nor time, nor place,
> Nor life, nor death can part.[8]
> —Charles Wesley

I've seen people go through hard, painful times and withdraw from others in the body of Christ. I've seen them pull away from the care, the support, the accountability of Christian community. I've seen them wither like a branch cut off from the Living Vine (see John 15:5-6). But I've also seen people face equally terrifying times and go deeper into their faith. I've seen them open their lives more fully to the presence of Christ in community with others. And I've seen them find the power to see it through.

The gaping hole at our younger daughter's wedding was the groom's younger brother who had been killed in a car accident five years before. As the family celebrated the joy of one son's wedding, they could not help but feel the other son's absence.

Across the years since their son's death, I had watched his parents deal with this worst of losses. They could have withdrawn. They could have pulled away from their faith. Instead, they drew closer to the church family that surrounded them. They opened their lives to the care, love, and strength of others. The depth of their pain drove them deeper into their faith. Instead of becoming bitter, they became better.

Wherever you are and whatever it is you are facing, the good news is that you don't have to face it alone. In the body of Christ, when one suffers, all suffer. When one rejoices, all rejoice. The choice is yours.

Your Reflections

- Describe a powerful face-to-face meeting you had with a person or group of people. Now imagine what it would have been like if you had experienced it virtually. List the ways in which it would have been different and what you would have missed. Write your thoughts below.

  I worked with a group of young people who came to our church to lead a Reach Work Camp. They were hard working an inspirational and I could have missed it if I didn't get involved

- Reflect on a time when you were facing something that was hard and painful. Write about it here. Did you withdraw from community, or were you supported by community?

  I had a difficult time with one member of our Lions club & my wife & other members supported me & it help me move on.

A Disciple's Heart: Daily Workbook

- If you were engaged in a faith community during the hard time you described above, describe the ways in which the community was present. If they were not present, write how their support might have made a difference.

  The men's group and other friends supported me & it helped.

- If you are currently in a season of hardship, how might you take a risk of sharing your hardship in community?

Your Guide to Prayer and Action

Lord Jesus Christ, give me the power to traverse the painful situations in my life now—those from the past that may be hindering me in the present, and those that will come to me in the future. Strengthen my participation in the body of Christ in this day and all the days of my life. Amen.

- Pray through 1 Corinthians 12:12-27 using *Lectio Divina* (refer to the steps on page 119). Whatever word or phrase God gives you from the Scripture during this time, use it throughout the day to center your thoughts.
- If you know about a friend or community member who is going through something difficult, reach out and schedule a face-to-face contact. Ask how you can be present for him or her.
- Create intentional space in your day to spend time in Christ's presence in the way in which you most enjoy (silence, music, singing, and so forth).

Week 4: Day 3
The Sacrament of Friendship

Scripture Reading
Read John 15:1-17.

Today's Message

As disciples of Jesus Christ, we are to follow his example in every area of life. It was this desire for holiness that drew Wesley and his followers together in the Holy Club.

While visiting Durham Cathedral in England, I became acquainted with a twelfth-century saint named Aelred, who is best remembered for his work on "Spiritual Friendship." He wrote to counter the common monastic idea that individual friendships were incompatible with devotion to Christ. Aelred said that taking pleasure in the company of friends was, in fact, an expression of the highest degree of Christian perfection. He specifically referred to the Gospel reading for today in which Jesus said that his disciples are no longer "servants" but "friends" (John 15:15).

Although the church has never named friendship as a sacrament, I believe that Jesus' words around the Last Supper table raise it to a sacramental level—an outward and tangible sign of the inward and spiritual grace. I sometimes think that friendship is the most overlooked Christian virtue, the most easily forgotten work of the Holy Spirit, and the most often neglected means of grace.

Friends are people who enjoy one another's company. As I think about my own closest friends, I realize that I smile when they come through the door. We laugh a lot. We enjoy the time we are together.

> Pour into our hearts, O God, the Holy Spirit's gift of love, that we, clasping each the other's hand, may share the joy of friendship, human and divine.[9]
> —Collect for St. Aelred Day

My guess is that the disciples might have said the same thing about Jesus. Walking with him beside the seashore, telling stories on the hillside, celebrating at a wedding party, or weeping beside his best friend's grave—just being in Jesus' presence could convert the ordinary disappointments and the ghastly dead ends of life into moments that were alive with the joy and freshness of eternal life. People were drawn to Jesus because they enjoyed being his in presence. Christ-centered friendship is like that.

Friends also are people who help each other. It's a mutual relationship that works both ways. It's what Paul was describing when he wrote, "[God] helps us in all our troubles, so that we are able to help others who have all kinds of troubles, using the same help that we ourselves have received from God" (2 Corinthians 1:4 GNT). I know that I am a more faithful disciple because I share the journey of discipleship with other disciples who encourage me in my weakness and hold me accountable to commitment to Christ.

I heard about a Sunday school teacher who asked the children to share how they felt about Jesus. One said, "If I asked Jesus if he loved me, he probably wouldn't answer me. He would just send me another kid to play with. He does things like that." Jesus does things like that through the grace of friendship.

Aristotle said that friends are people with whom we share a moral vision. The members of the Holy Club were drawn together by a common vision of life that flowed from a heart that was being made perfect or complete in the love of God in Jesus Christ. I'm aware that my closest friends are people who share a common vision of a life that is centered in Christ.

One of the memorable stories of friendship in our nation's history was the relationship between Thomas Jefferson and John Adams. Despite their close friendship during the Revolution, they became alienated from each other after Jefferson became president. Finally, in 1811, one of Jefferson's neighbors told him that he had heard Adams say, "I always loved Jefferson, and still love him." In response Jefferson wrote, "This is enough for me. I only needed this knowledge to revive towards him all of the affections of the most cordial moments of our lives."[10] He reflected on the way they had come through the troubled seas of the Revolution together. Although separated by politics and geography, they were inseparably bound together in the vision that gave birth to this nation.

Likewise, Christian friends are bound together in Jesus' vision of the kingdom of God. They dare to live as if they actually believe that God's kingdom of wholeness, justice, freedom, and peace is being fulfilled on earth as it is in heaven. Even death cannot break the bond between Christian friends, for they know that one day they are bound together in the everlasting love of God. In Christ, they share a bond that cannot be broken.

Saint Aelred got it right. Friendship is not a contradiction of the Christian life but a vital tool that the Holy Spirit uses to perfect us in love. Disciples continue to grow in their discipleship because they share Christ-centered friendship with other disciples. Even as the bread and cup become the outward and visible sign of God's inward and spiritual grace in Holy Communion, Christian friendship becomes a tangible expression of the love of God that became flesh in Jesus becoming flesh in us.

> If death my friend and me divide,
> Thou dost not, Lord, my sorrow chide,
> Or frown my tears to see;
> Restrained from passionate excess,
> Thou bidst me mourn in calm distress
> For them that rest in Thee.
>
> I feel a strong immortal hope,
> Which bears my mournful spirit up
> Beneath its mountain load;
> Redeemed from death, and grief, and pain,
> I soon shall find my friend again
> Within the arms of God.[11]
> —Charles Wesley

Your Reflections

- How does knowing that Jesus calls you "friend" change your understanding of your relationship with God?

It gives me more confidence that have the Holy Spirit here to help me

- Who are the friends with whom you most enjoy spending time? How have they helped you be your best self?

My wife, #1 helps me do the the things I worry about.

- Name some of the people with whom you share a "moral vision" or a life that is centering on loving God and loving others? How can you cultivate these relationships today?

Doug Campbell, John Smith, Joe Payne, Ed Heally
I need to find more time to share God's guidance with these men.

Your Guide to Prayer and Action

Loving God, I give thanks for the gift of friendship—for those friends in my past, those current friendships that give me hope, and the ones that will come in the future. Shape these divine relationships into ones that will blossom through trial, disagreement, and all of life's transitions. May they reflect the divine commitment you make to me reflected in Jesus' life, death, and resurrection. Amen.

- Pray through John 15:1-17 using *Lectio Divina* (refer to the steps on page 119). Whatever word or phrase God gives you from the Scripture during this time, use it throughout the day to center your thoughts.
- Pray for the person you consider to be your closest spiritual friend. Contact this person to share how much he or she means to you.
- Each day this week, pray for a friend or former friend with whom you are in conflict. Discern through prayer whether you are to reach out and attempt to reconcile.

A Disciple's Heart: Daily Workbook

Week 4: Day 4
The Imperfect Way to Perfection

Scripture Reading

Read Romans 1:1-7.

Today's Message

The journey toward perfection is never perfect, particularly when we make that journey in the company of other imperfect disciples in the imperfect community we call the church. A popular version of an old Irish ditty says this:

> To be there above
> With the saints that we love—
> That will be glory!
>
> But to be here below
> With the saints that we know—
> That's another story!

It's one thing to celebrate John's vision of the church in heaven as the pure and perfect "Bride of Christ" (Revelation 19:7-9). But it's something else to actually live and serve in the church on earth, which is always less than perfect because it is made up of people who have not reached perfection yet.

It's not that there is anything new to this. I'm sure the folks in Rome were more than a little surprised to hear Paul address them as "God's beloved in Rome, who are called to be saints" (Romans 1:7 NRSV). They must have said, "Called to be saints? You've got to be kidding. That's just a little beyond my pay grade." How many times have you heard someone say, "Well, I'm no saint . . . "? How many times have you said that yourself?

But isn't there something inside of us that wants to say, "Wow. It may not be who I am, but it's something I wouldn't mind becoming"? Isn't there something inside of us that would like to reach a little farther or climb a little higher? Isn't there something about the New Testament vision for the church that is worth our investment?

Life in the church reminds me of the preamble to the Constitution for the United States that says we are here "to form a more perfect union." Living into that union is no small task. Living into sainthood in the company of other sinners is never easy. But Paul consistently used two words that provide the master keys to open the door that leads to Christian perfection.

The first word is *love*. Paul called the folks in Rome "God's beloved." He told the Ephesians, "God who is rich in mercy, out of the great love with which he has loved us . . . made us alive together with

Christ" (Ephesians 2:4-5 NRSV). Other communities in the Christian family may find their starting point in other aspects of God's character revealed in Scripture, but in the Wesleyan tradition, the dynamic center is always God's love.

It's not love the way the world understands it. It's not the love of puppies, the love of country, or love for your favorite football team. It's the unique, one-and-only love that is defined by the life, death, and resurrection of Jesus. It's the love that loves us when we are unlovable. It's the love that went all the way to the cross.

Justin remembers a woman who contacted him after recently coming back to church. She shared with him that she had been pregnant and the father of the child had expressed that he didn't want the baby. Soon after she had found out that she was pregnant, she had had a miscarriage. As they talked about her life and her grief, she said that she believed that God was punishing her for an abortion she had when she was young. Justin reminded her that God called her "beloved" in spite of any mistakes in the past, and that God wept with her as she lost her child. He affirmed God had forgiven her—that God loves her. She wept as she experienced the depth of God's love.

The second word is *grace*. Paul opens his letter to the Romans with his favorite greeting, "Grace to you and peace from God our Father and the Lord Jesus Christ" (Romans 1:7). He uses the word three times in two sentences in his letter to the Christians in Ephesus:

> By **grace** you have been saved . . . so that in the ages to come he might show the immeasurable riches of his **grace** in kindness toward us in Christ Jesus. For by **grace** you have been saved through faith, and this is not your own doing; it is the gift of God—not the result of works, so that no one may boast." (Ephesians 2:5-9 NRSV, emphasis added)

I know a young man who grew up in a very conservative Christian home. He obeyed the rules, did what everyone expected him to do, married the young woman everyone expected him to marry, and even served on a ministry staff. But finally the day came when he could live the lie no longer. After years of prayer and counseling, he accepted the fact that he is gay. He was immediately excluded from his church and alienated from his family. He thought there was no place for him in the community of faith until a friend invited him to his congregation. With differing individual convictions regarding the church's understanding of homosexuality, the people extended God's grace and acceptance to this young man in tangible and surprising ways. He gave thanks for the way the church helped heal his broken heart. In time, he was reconciled with his family, and he is continuing to make the journey toward perfection.

From beginning to end, the journey toward perfection in our individual lives and in the life of the church is grounded in the love and grace of God in Jesus Christ. We are meant to live together in a community of love and grace. The question for us is this: Why would we settle for anything less?

Your Reflections

- Describe a time in your life when you felt that you were far from God.

  At times when I was tempted to do something I knew was wrong. But even then I felt he was forgiving and caring for me.

- Have you been able to transition from experiencing distance from God to experiencing God calling you "beloved"? If so, how?

  Through prayer & asking for forgiveness

- How are you experiencing the "immeasurable riches of his grace in kindness toward you in Christ Jesus" in your life right now?

  Through my friends, family & men's group

- How have you seen or experienced the love and grace of God at work in your faith community or small group?

  Yes in both.   Food distribution, Habitat, Liens

Your Guide to Prayer and Action

God, help me believe that I am a saint. Give me the power to live today knowing that even though I am an unfinished disciple and cling to some of my character defects and imperfections, your grace covers me. May I heed the call to live in spiritual community and to love others deeply. May I see that it is by my imperfections that you will use me to participate in your transformation of this world as I prepare for the next. Amen.

- Pray through Romans 1:1-7 using *Lectio Divina* (refer to the steps on page 119). Whatever word or phrase God gives you from the Scripture during this time, use it throughout the day to center your thoughts.
- Think of an imperfection or defect of character that seems to foster conflict with others. How can you invite God into it today?

WEEK 4: DAY 5
WE'RE ALL IN THE SAME BOAT

Scripture Readings

Read Psalm 46 and Mark 4:35-41.

Today's Message

It's no wonder the disciples were frightened when "gale-force winds arose, and waves crashed against the boat so that the boat was swamped" (Mark 4:37). In his painting "The Storm on the Sea of Galilee," Rembrandt captured the moment when the boat was about to sink. (You can search the title online for an image of the painting.) One disciple, hanging onto the ropes, looks out toward us with helpless fear on his face. Art historians say it is the face of the artist. Rembrandt put himself into the boat in the middle of the storm.

Like Rembrandt, sooner or later every one of us will find ourselves in the storm. When Jesus told the parable of the wise and foolish builders (Matthew 7:24-27), he used the same words to describe the storm that blew against each of their houses. The difference was not in the strength of the storm but in the strength of the foundation upon which their houses were built.

The point is that everyone faces storms. They come in different ways with different names and at different times, but the storms will come. The critical question for the life of faith is not whether we can escape the storm, but whether we will have nurtured the kind of faith that will see us through it.

I don't agree with the promises of the "prosperity gospel" that if we have faith we will be given immunity from the hurt, pain, and disappointments of this world and get rich at the same time. Nor do I agree with the belief that God has a reason for *every* painful thing that happens to us. Storms simply happen, and any of us can get caught up in them. But I do believe that in the same way Jesus was with the disciples in that storm-tossed boat on the Sea of Galilee, so his Spirit is with us in the storm. There was nothing unusual about fishermen getting caught in a storm. What makes this story different is that Jesus was in the boat with them.

The disciples woke Jesus with the question, "Teacher, don't you care that we're drowning?" (Mark 4:38). They thought Jesus didn't care. The truth is that Jesus wasn't afraid. "He got up and gave orders to the winds, and he said to the lake, 'Silence! Be still!' The wind settled down and there was a great calm" (Mark 4:39). In that quiet place in the middle of the storm, Jesus asked the tough question: "Why are you frightened? Don't you have faith yet?" (Mark 4:40).

The question is not whether the storms will come. It's whether we will have the faith to face them. The question is not whether the winds will blow. It's whether we will have nurtured the kind of relationship with Christ that enables us to stay calm when they blow. The question is not whether our house will shake. It's whether we have built a strong enough foundation for it to stand. The critical question is whether Jesus has become for us a calm place in the eye of the storm.

A Disciple's Heart: Daily Workbook

I wonder if Mark had Psalm 46 in mind when he wrote this story about the disciples and Jesus in the storm (NRSV):

> God is our refuge and strength,
>   a very present help in trouble.
> Therefore we will not fear, though the earth should change,
>   though the mountains shake in the heart of the sea;
> though its waters roar and foam,
>   though the mountains tremble with its tumult. . . .
> "Be still, and know that I am God! . . . "
> The Lord of hosts is with us;
>   the God of Jacob is our refuge.

The good news is not that we will be protected from every storm but that we can always know the presence of God in the midst of the storm. Jesus' question haunts us: "Don't you have faith yet?"

The kind of faith that can see us through the storm is not something we pick up at the home improvement store along with plywood and duct tape when the wind starts to blow and the rain starts to fall. It's not something we grab at the last minute when we are told to evacuate.

The faith that sees us through the storm is nurtured over time. It is born out of deep wrestling with Scripture and quiet hours of prayer. It matures in community with other disciples who encourage, support, and challenge us. It is the result of the practice of spiritual disciplines in the calm days of our lives so that we can draw on it in the middle of the storm.

Did you know that throughout church history, the ship or boat has been one of the basic visual metaphors for the church? That's why the central part of the church building where disciples gather for worship has traditionally been called the *nave*—the seventeenth century Latin word for *ship*. To be part of the body of Christ, to share life together in "the Company of the Committed," means that we are all in the same boat. And the Spirit of the One who calmed the storm on the Sea of Galilee is in the boat with us. May he be so deeply alive in us that we may share his calm in the midst of every storm.

Your Reflections

- Remember a time when you yelled out to God in the storm and perceived God to be uncaring or indifferent. Describe the situation.

  ② When we learned that our grandson was autistic

  ① when my father got cancer

- Were you practicing the spiritual disciplines prior to entering that storm? Why or why not? What was going on in your life at the time?

① No I was busy working & not part of a church family
② Yes I was part of this church family

- When have you been in the ship with other disciples (or family) during a storm and felt extremely scared?

No

- How are you nurturing your faith amidst the storms of life?

Prayer & being part of a church family & small group

Your Guide to Prayer and Action

God, I thank you for being with me in the storms of my life. While it is hard to understand the why, I know you are there with me. May I be present for others while they are in the midst of a storm, remembering that you will never leave us. Amen.

- Pray through Psalm 46 or Mark 4:35-41 using *Lectio Divina* (refer to the steps on page 119). Whatever word or phrase God gives you from the Scripture during this time, use it throughout the day to center your thoughts.
- Sit comfortably in a chair in a quiet place. Gently close your eyes and repeat the phrase "Be still and know that I am God" for five minutes. Write about your experience in a journal.
- Recalling the storm you identified in Your Reflections, write a letter to yourself from the future providing perspective about how you will get through the storm and the ways in which it will strengthen your faith. Use a journal or writing paper.

A Disciple's Heart: Daily Workbook

WEEK 5
ON FIRE WITH HOLY LOVE

Sanctification is not just about us. Being made perfect in love includes the process by which the Holy Spirit empowers us to be the agents of God's love and grace in the world. The aim of Christian perfection is both a warm heart and a transformed world. Discipleship in the Wesleyan tradition always combines the inner life of personal piety with the outward witness of social action and an evangelistic passion to draw other people into the journey of discipleship.

The combination of inner spiritual growth and outward service is the result of a heart "strangely warmed" by the passionate fire of divine love. The prophet Jeremiah described it as a fire in his bones that he could not put out (Jeremiah 20:9). The danger is that somewhere along the way we allow that fire to grow dim. John Wesley left us this warning:

> I am not afraid that the people called Methodists should ever cease to exist either
> in Europe or America. But I am afraid lest they should only exist as a dead sect,
> having the form of religion without the power. And this undoubtedly will be the
> case unless they hold fast the doctrine, spirit, and discipline with which they first
> set out.[1]

Imbedded in Wesley's warning are three necessary elements of discipleship that can keep the fire of divine love burning: doctrine, discipline, and spirit.

Wesleyan *doctrine* reminds us of who we are and why we are here—our mission. It's doctrine that is centered in the love of God. It's a way of making disciples that is patterned after Wesley's understanding of the grace that meets us wherever we are but loves us too much to leave us there. It's a lifelong journey of sanctification that never quits forming us into people who love God and love others. It's a life of servanthood that sends us into the world, not to condemn the world but to participate in God's transformation of it.

Wesleyan *discipline* defines the way we accomplish our mission. By *discipline* I mean something much deeper than a legalistic obedience to external rules. I'm thinking of the spiritual disciplines by which our hearts, minds, and actions are formed into the likeness of the love of God in Christ and empowered for transformative ministry in the world.

> Enlarge, inflame, and fill my heart
> With boundless charity divine,
> So shall I all my strength exert,
> And love them with a zeal like thine.[2]
> —Charles Wesley

If our *doctrine* reminds us of our mission and our *discipline* defines method, it's the *spirit* of divine love that keeps the fire burning. In the Wesleyan tradition, knowing what is right is never enough. The truth must always be expressed in active service to others that is energized and directed by the Spirit of God.

This week we explore some of the ways the Spirit of God energizes Wesleyan disciples for witness and service. Our hope is that the Spirit will rekindle within each of us the fire of divine love and send us into the world as the agents of God's kingdom coming on earth as it is in heaven.

A Disciple's Heart: Daily Workbook

WEEK 5: DAY 1
STIR UP THE FIRE

Scripture Reading

Read 2 Timothy 1:1-7.

Today's Message

Every disciple should have a mentor like Paul. In today's reading the apostle is writing to his young protégé, Timothy, to remind him of his calling and to encourage him in his ministry. He challenges Timothy to "rekindle the gift of God that is within you through the laying on of my hands" (2 Timothy 1:6 NRSV). J.B. Phillips paraphrased that verse to read, "Stir up that inner fire which God gave you."

Fellow pastor Magrey deVega has pointed out that the Greek verb used in this verse, *anazopureo*, comes from three root words: *Ana*, meaning "up," *Pyreo*, meaning "fire," and *Zo-on*, which can mean "beast." Based on this knowledge, he has created his own personal paraphrase of Paul's words: "Wake up the fire-breathing beast within you!"[3]

I can hear Paul saying, "I know it's still there. You received it from your grandmother and your mother. I know that it has been lulled to sleep by the hard work of ministry, the petty nitpicking of some of the people you've had to put up with, but it's time for you to wake up the fire-breathing beast within you so that you can fulfill your mission."

Like Timothy, the faith was passed down to me from my parents and grandparents. They provided the kindling for the fire. But my experience at summer youth camps ignited the flames.

One summer at an old-fashioned Methodist camp meeting I experienced an adolescent romance. The after-camp relationship lasted long enough for us to get together one day at the county fair. I remember walking along the midway with its tents that invited us to experience all sorts of exotic things. One promised "The Wild Man of the Jungle" with a colorful painting of a fierce-looking man with bulging muscles wrestling with a gigantic alligator.

We paid a quarter and went inside only to find a gray-headed old man who looked like he had had more than enough to drink the night before. He was sitting in the dust, fumbling around with a few harmless garden snakes.

My immediate thought was, "What a rip off!" I was just about to say something I probably would have regretted when she turned to me and said, "Just think, Jim. This is a man for whom Christ died." It was one time when I knew enough to keep my mouth shut. That fact had never entered my mind.

The summer romance ended before the autumn leaves fell from the trees, but the memory of the way the love of Christ had enabled her to see that old man through the eyes of Christ continues to

> "Are you better instructed than to put asunder what God has joined? Than to separate works of piety from works of mercy? Are you uniformly zealous of both?"[4]
> —John Wesley

lead me in the direction of being made perfect in love in the way I relate to every person.

Many years later I experienced another dimension of that same love in the witness of Peter Storey, who led the Methodist Church of Southern Africa in the struggle against apartheid. His courageous leadership grew out of his conviction that for John Wesley "this love of God and man was neither a feeling, nor even a noun, but always a verb."[5] Love is not always something we feel; it is something we do. It is the way we become God's change-agents in confronting the systems and powers that demean people, destroy lives, and damage the environment in a sin-infected world.

Wesley's "General Rules" put the love of Christ into concrete action with a few simple verbs:

- "Doing no harm, by avoiding evil of every kind."
- "By doing good; by being in every kind merciful after their power; as they have opportunity, doing good of every possible sort, and, as far as possible, to all men."
- "By attending upon all the ordinances of God" including worship, Scripture, Holy Communion, prayer, and fasting.[6]

In recent years, Bishop Reuben Job re-presented these in *Three Simple Rules*: "1. Do no harm 2. Do good 3. Stay in love with God."[7]

Wesley knew that when it comes to actual transformation in the way we live, it's often more important to act our way into a new way of feeling than to try to feel our way into a new way of acting. He called his followers to practical behaviors that, if practiced over time, become the tangible expression of the intangible love of God that was revealed in Christ. Another way of saying this is that if holiness does not begin in the heart, it never begins. But if it ends in the heart and is never transformed into action, it ends.

The old spiritual prays, "Lord, I want to be more loving in my heart."[8] The challenge for every disciple is to allow the Spirit of God to "stir up the fire-breathing beast" so that each of us in our own unique way will participate in God's transformation in the world.

Your Reflections

- Who are the people who have instilled faith in you like Timothy's mother and grandmother?

Rev Boyton, Mom, Aunt Vesta, Grandma O'Hara

- Is there a fire in you that has been "lulled to sleep" and needs to be rekindled or stirred up? If so, what is it? *I need to reach out to my children, any friends & those in need.*

- How are you practicing the "simple rules" by doing no harm, doing good, and staying in love with God? Which rule is the most challenging for you? *My work w habitat & Lions Club & Food dist. help me to serve do good. I some time get angry & speak before I think*

- How has the fire of God's love transformed the way you see other people? The way you see the world in which you live? *I try to realize that other also make mistake & that I should love & care for them & not Judge them. The same applies for the rest of the world.*

Your Guide to Prayer and Action

Collect for St. Bernard of Clairvaux (1090–1153)

O God, by whose grace your servant Bernard of Clairvaux, Kindled with the flame of your love, became a burning and a shining light in your Church: Grant that we also may be aflame with the spirit of love and discipline, and walk before you as children of light; through Jesus Christ our Lord, who lives and reigns with you in the unity of the Holy Spirit, one God, now and for ever. Amen.[9]

- Follow the instructions on page 120 for a time of centering prayer. Read aloud 2 Timothy 1:1-7 to begin your prayer period, or use another passage of your own choosing.
- Wesley's "General Rules" provide a common heritage for the churches of denominations in the Methodist tradition. Find them on the Internet and see how they speak to you (see http://archives.umc.org/interior.asp?mid=1648).
- Write a letter to one or more of the mentors who have influenced your life of faith—or have a personal conversation. Give thanks for the way each person has impacted your life.

Week 5: Day 2
Contagious Christians

Scripture Reading
Read Luke 2:8-20.

Today's Message
If the Christian faith were like a case of the flu, would anyone be at risk of catching it from you? Just how contagious are you?

John Wesley believed that a sure sign that a person is growing toward Christian perfection is a heart-burning passion to share the love of God with others. He wrote, "The more they are filled with the life of God, the more tenderly will they be concerned for those who are still without God in the world."[10]

Today's Scripture invites us into the story of the least likely people who became amazingly effective in sharing the good news of God's love in Christ.

We know so little about them, but we know that shepherds were social outcasts. They were at the bottom of everyone's social ladder. To the Greeks, they were irresponsible thieves who grazed their sheep on other people's land. To the Jews, they were "unclean" because there was no way for them to obey the rules about food and cleanliness. Spend enough time with sheep in the wilderness and you will start to smell like them. These shepherds were nobodies, social rejects, absolutely the least likely people to get in on any big news or to be credible witnesses of it.

We meet them "in the fields, guarding their sheep at night" (Luke 2:8). Suddenly, the darkness to which they had become all too accustomed was shattered. "The Lord's angel stood before them, the Lord's glory shone around them, and they were terrified" (Luke 2:9).

You'd be terrified too. In the Gospels, angels show up as an unexpected and often unwanted intrusion into the ordinary patterns of life. They're like a television reporter who interrupts the most critical play of the football game with breaking news of a major event. Like a good reporter, angels never draw attention to what they are doing; they turn our attention toward what God is doing.

"I bring good news to you—wonderful, joyous news for all people. Your savior is born today." The angel then points these least likely of witnesses to the least likely of places. "You will find a newborn baby wrapped snugly and lying in a manger" (Luke 2:10-12).

What would you do with news like that? Luke says the shepherds did the least likely thing you can imagine. They left their flocks in the field—which, in terms of their economic stability, was a very risky thing to do—and hurried off to Bethlehem.

They found what they were looking for and did the least likely thing: "They reported what they had been told about this child. Everyone who heard it was amazed at what the shepherds told them" (Luke 2:17-18).

A Disciple's Heart: Daily Workbook

We'd call what happened through the shepherds "viral communication." Their story "went viral." It became "contagious."

There was something downright contagious about the good news that the Savior had come. So contagious that people accepted the good news even when it came from the shepherds. That's how it works today too.

Justin remembers an unlikely messenger who brought the contagious good news into his life:

> In my sophomore year of college, we were suspended from our fraternity house and moved to an apartment complex where I met a security guard who became a shepherd of sorts to me—even though I didn't understand it at the time. I was living far from God, stuck in addiction and unhealthy living. He sensed that I had a lot of pain undergirding my behavior, and he displayed a presence and kindness I had not experienced since my childhood. He once even stuck his neck out for me when I caused a disturbance in the complex. He shared that he was once like me and that his relationship with Christ changed the direction of his life. He invited me to his church a number of times. He was not pushy but offered a different way of living, but I rebutted all of his invitations. Toward the end of the semester he told me that he was leaving the security job to become a pastor. Over the summer he wrote me letters, sharing words of encouragement and saying that he was praying for me. He was a contagious shepherd with the good news of Jesus Christ. He will probably never know the way God's preventing grace was at work through him. Yet I will never forget the way that he shared the contagious good news of Jesus Christ.

The good news the shepherds shared was contagious because Jesus saves us from . . .

- the deadly virus of self-centeredness by the good infection of love for God and for others.
- the contagion of greed by infecting us with generosity.
- the contamination of racism, bigotry, and perverted patriotism by infecting us with a vision for social justice.
- the bacteria of fear by infecting us with confidence in the goodness of God.
- our diseased addiction to violence by infecting us with a vision of peace.
- the virus of despair by infecting us with hope.

> "[Jesus] came to this world and became a man in order to spread to other men the kind of life He has—by what I call 'good infection.' Every Christian is to become a little Christ. The whole purpose of becoming a Christian is simply nothing else."[11]
> —C. S. Lewis

- our self-destructive sin by taking our infection into himself and dying on the cross.
- the lethal power of death by rising from the dead and infecting us with the promise of everlasting life.

Now that's good news! No wonder the shepherds became contagious in sharing it. You are a disciple of Jesus Christ because across the centuries messengers like these shepherds have passed the "good infection" down from generation to generation. Someone passed it on to you. Now you have the opportunity to become contagious in passing it on to someone else.

So, if the love of God in Christ were like a good case of the flu, would anyone need to worry about catching it from you? Just how contagious are you?

Your Reflections

- Has an unlikely messenger ever shown up and given you good news? If so, describe the experience briefly.

- Who would your community identify as the outcasts?

  Gays
  Muslims
  Hooded black youth

- Who have you labeled as an outcast in your mind? How might you share the good news with them?

  Far right conservatives
  God loves us all

A Disciple's Heart: Daily Workbook

- Reflect on your experience of growing in Christ. What would you say is contagious about your spiritual journey? What can other people see and experience in your life that would represent Christ's love? What could other people catch from you?

> My service to those in need
> My tolerance for others positions
> My love of Jesus

Your Guide to Prayer and Action

God, open my ears and eyes today to the reality that there could be "shepherds" around me, unlikely messengers waiting to give me good news. Prompt me to be a contagious shepherd who shares your love with those who are easy to love and those who are not. Give me boldness combined with a gentle spirit so that I am a bearer of the good news this week. Amen.

- Follow the instructions on page 120 for a time of centering prayer. Read aloud Luke 2:8-20 to begin your prayer period, or use another passage of your own choosing.
- Ask God to guide you to become contagious with your faith in ways that are consistent with who you are.

WEEK 5: DAY 3
A FLOWER IN THE JUNKYARD

Scripture Reading
Read Isaiah 58:1-14.

Today's Message

On a train ride through a major city I had a close-up view of a junkyard, complete with rusting machinery and broken-down cars. But as I looked more closely, I noticed the green vines of Confederate Jasmine growing up through the junk. The buds were just about ready to open. In time, the ugly reality of the junkyard would be soaked in the perfume of their snow-white blossoms. It reminded me of the way Jesus said the kingdom of God grows in this world like a mustard seed (Matthew 13:31-32).

I've held the memory of those flowers in the junkyard as a visual image of the way God's kingdom is relentlessly growing amid the junk of a sin-broken world. It could also be a metaphor for the way that the love being perfected in our hearts begins to impact the structures and systems of this world, which stand in need of God's redemption. The term we often use to describe that impact is *social justice*.

Like any good word or phrase, the term *social justice* can be distorted into something that is alien to the spirit of the Gospels. The problem is that the theme of God's vision of social justice is so deeply woven into Scripture that when you try to pull it out, the whole thing starts to unravel.

The Hebrew word *mishpat* appears over four hundred times in the Old Testament. A basic definition is "the restoration of a situation or environment which promoted equity and harmony (*shalom*) in a community."[12] In the New Testament, Jesus inaugurates his ministry with the prophetic vision of justice from Isaiah:

> *The Spirit of the Lord is upon me,*
> *because the Lord has anointed me.*
> *He has sent me to preach good news to the poor,*
> *to proclaim release to the prisoners*
> *and recovery of sight to the blind,*
> *to liberate the oppressed,*
> *and to proclaim the year of the Lord's favor. (Luke 4:18-19)*

Jesus' parables of the Kingdom and Matthew's collection of his teaching, which we know as the Sermon on the Mount, are rooted in the promise of God's justice and righteousness being worked out in human experience. Paul compares the fulfillment of God's redemption of this world

A Disciple's Heart: Daily Workbook

to a woman in labor, waiting with eager longing for the new creation to be born. The grand finale of Scripture in Revelation can be read as John's Technicolor vision of the way God's justice will ultimately be fulfilled in the whole creation.

In the eighteenth century, Wesley didn't use the term *social justice*, but the vision for God's mercy and justice has been an active part of the Wesleyan tradition ever since the members of the Holy Club began visiting in prisons, workhouses, and orphanages. Wesley campaigned for prison reform and challenged the early Methodists to be engaged with the poor. He encouraged William Wilberforce, who called for the abolition of slavery in the British Empire. Methodists in America worked for women's voting rights, child labor laws, Prohibition, and racial justice. Methodists in South Africa participated in the struggle against apartheid.

Equally faithful disciples sometimes hold differing convictions about the ways the biblical vision of social justice is applied to specific situations, but the mandate for followers of Christ to be actively engaged in the transformation of the kingdoms of this earth into the kingdom of God is relentlessly present across church history. It is the way we become the answer to the prayer that God's kingdom will come and God's will be done on earth as it is in heaven.

Isaiah 58 is one of the most eloquent and disturbing passages in the Old Testament. It causes me to say that my problem with Scripture is not with the things I do not understand but with the things I understand clearly but don't want to obey.

> "To be the church, from a Wesleyan point of view, is to accept Jesus' invitation to participate in a new age of peace with justice founded upon the reckless abandonment of power and self."[13]
> —Paul Wesley Chilcote

The prophet goes after the covenant people for maintaining their religious practices (fasting in particular) while ignoring the needs of people around them. But God's word of judgment becomes a magnificent word of promise as the prophet describes how wonderful life can be when we act in ways that are consistent with the heart of the God we worship.

I love Isaiah's promise that if God's people act in ways that are consistent with God's love and justice, "[we] shall be called the repairer of the breach, the restorer of streets to live in" (Isaiah 58:12 NRSV). We could use some Spirit-led "repairers of the breach" in our politically, economically, and socially polarized country today.

The vision of Christian perfection is not only the transformation of individual lives but also the transformation of the whole creation. In our not-yet-perfect ways, every disciple is called to bear witness to the perfect vision of God's kingdom coming on earth as it is fulfilled in heaven. It is God's flower growing in the junkyard, assuring us that one day it will take over the whole place!

The TV show "Mission Impossible" opened with the words "Your mission, should you choose to accept it . . . " The mission for every disciple is to discover his or her own way to participate in God's work of *mishpat* in our personal relationships and in the world around us. Will you accept it?

Your Reflections

- How do you respond to the biblical definition of *social justice*? How have you seen injustice in the world around you?

  Our country has come a long toward Social Justice but has a ways to go. There are many children who don't have enough of the right food.

- Have you ever felt that you were maintaining religious practices but ignoring the needs of people around you? How did this realization come to you, and how did you respond?

  I have not done enough to reach out to help the poor & unchurched. I have worked with our food dist.

- What needs in the community is your faith community helping to meet? What other specific need is God calling you to address?

  Food distribution & housing. Doing more to connect with the unchurched

- How can you become a "repairer of the breach"?

  Reach out to the poor.

Your Guide to Prayer and Action

Triune God, may my faith community be a repairer of the breach. May we provide the nutrients for your flowers to grow in the junkyards of the world. May I continue my work to participate in your transformation of my community. Amen.

- Pray through Isaiah 58:1-14 using *Lectio Divina* (refer to the steps on page 119). Whatever word or phrase God gives you from the Scripture during this time, use it throughout the day to center your thoughts.
- Read through Isaiah 58, using a Bible commentary as a resource as you study.

A Disciple's Heart: Daily Workbook

WEEK 5: DAY 4
THE POWER OF ONE

Scripture Reading

Read 1 Samuel 25:1-35.

Today's Message

When her parents asked what she wanted for her sixth birthday, Emma told them she didn't want presents. She had heard that there are children who don't have shoes. Instead of receiving gifts for herself, she spread the word that she wanted to collect shoes for them. The next Sunday she tugged her red wagon into the sanctuary loaded down with fifty-five pairs of athletic shoes. A week later she had collected more than one hundred pairs of shoes.

With millions of children in poverty in our country and around the world, Emma's wagonload of shoes may not seem that it would make much of an impact. But don't tell that to the children who will have new shoes because of Emma. And don't tell her parents that collecting those shoes has not had a profound impact on Emma's life.

When we look at the aching needs of our world—hunger, poverty, war, disease, economic injustice, ethnic and political conflict—we can easily become overwhelmed. And when we add up the numbers of people who have not yet heard the good news, experienced the love of God, and become disciples of Jesus Christ, the task of making disciples for the transformation of the world can seem impossible. What impact can any one of us have?

It's like asking the question *How do you eat an elephant?* The answer is *One bite at a time.* Emma reminds us that lives are restored, people are saved, disciples are made, and the world is ultimately transformed through ordinary people who offer their lives as instruments of God's peace, love, and justice.

Emma's story demonstrates the way one life can make a difference. The same was true for Abigail, whose individual action prevented an unnecessary war. Her husband was a rich, arrogant man named Nabal. In Hebrew his name means "fool." David's knee-jerk reaction to Nabal's insult was to strap on the sword. Sadly, this is the all-too-typical response of leaders and nations in our sin-twisted, violence-addicted, conflict-prone world. Our first reaction is to send in the troops and fire up the drones. It proves the old adage that when the only tool in the toolbox is a hammer, everything looks like a nail.

If Abigail hadn't broken the cycle of violence by finding another way to resolve the crisis, there likely would have been a bloodbath that could have left a permanent stain on David's reputation and conscience.

> "For Wesleyan Christians there is no 'personal' Gospel, no 'social' Gospel: there is only the *whole* Gospel, expressed both personally and socially."[14]
> —Peter Storey

I'll grant that Abigail is a minority character in the Old Testament. David fought a lot of bloody battles. The "warring madness" of our sinful world continues to this day. But in Abigail we find the picture of a wise woman who made a difference by seeking a nonviolent way to resolve the conflict. She did what she could, and God used her efforts in ways that went beyond all expectations.

I suspect that some folks thought Abigail was foolish. But in the end, it turned out to be the foolish wisdom that saved the day. It was the foolishness of God's nonviolent way of dealing with evil that would later be revealed at a cross; the foolishness that Paul said "is wiser than human wisdom . . . stronger than human strength" (1 Corinthians 1:25 NRSV).

Jesus compared the presence of the kingdom of God in this world to small things that make a big difference: mustard seeds planted in the ground, leaven in a loaf of bread, a candle burning in the darkness. His parables are vivid reminders that often the transformation of the kingdoms of this world into the kingdom of God happens through individuals like Emma and Abigail who do what they can to make a difference, believing that God is able to use those efforts in ways that go far beyond anything we can imagine (see Ephesians 3:20).

In many ways, Emma and Abigail could not be farther apart. But in one way, they share the common witness of one faithful person doing what he or she can as an agent of God's love in a broken and hurting world. Their witness is an invitation for each of us to see the opportunities that God gives us to be the agents of his love, compassion, justice, and peace.

Your Reflections

- Name a person whom you admire because, like Emma, he or she responded to a need in your community. Describe what this person did to make a difference.

  Aubrey Smith started our food collection at the grocery stores with $100 that Pastor John gave him to use wisely

- Reflect on and share the ways you are living the "whole" gospel—that is, living it both personally and socially. *I work with Habitat for Humanity to raise money & build homes for those in need*

A Disciple's Heart: Daily Workbook

- Who is the Abigail in your life? Who has given you wisdom counter to the world's wisdom that saved your day? *My mother who was a elementry school teacha*

- Is there a person in your life whom you could prevent from making a foolish mistake by providing wise counsel? *My children*

Your Guide to Prayer and Action

Christ Jesus, may I remember the power of one—the one life I have to share. May I live the foolishness of the nonviolence today in my mind and in my heart. If I feel anger or fear, may it be transformed for good. In the name of the Father, Son, and Holy Spirit. Amen.

- Pray through 1 Samuel 25:1-35 using *Lectio Divina* (refer to the steps on page 119). Whatever word or phrase God gives you from the Scripture during this time, use it throughout the day to center your thoughts.
- Develop a prayer or action plan that will help you to live the whole gospel—personally and socially. Write your ideas below.

Heavenly father guide me that I might reach out to my children and to others in need of Christ in there lives

- Write a note of gratitude and send it to the person in your life who is like Abigail. Share how this person has impacted your life.
- Reach out to the person you identified who could use wise counsel. If there is currently not such a person in your life, pray for the Spirit to reveal an opportunity for you to give wise counsel.

Week 5: Day 5
Daring to Be Extremely Christian

Scripture Reading
Read 1 Corinthians 1:18–2:2.

Today's Message

Turn on the TV or read the news and you will see the invidious impact of political and religious extremism in our world today. According to the New Testament, there is only one kind of extremism that bears witness to Christ, and it is the extremism of love—love for God, love for others, love for the world, and love for those we call enemies. You can't get more extreme than that.

Scott Jones describes the Wesleyn tradition as the "extreme center."[15] It sounds like an oxymoron. How can something be both extreme, meaning "the point located farthest from the middle," and *center*? Only a fool would believe something like that!

That is exactly what the Apostle Paul told the Corinthians. He used the Greek word *moria*, from which we get the word *moron*, to say that the cross is foolishness to the world. Nothing could be further from the mundane middle of things than the offensive, shocking, subversive extremism of God's love at the cross. But that is precisely the "living center" around which the Christian life revolves.

There is a lot about the words and way of Jesus that, by the world's standards, sounds downright foolish. Jesus begins the Sermon on the Mount with these words:

> *Blessed are the poor in spirit . . .*
> *Blessed are those who mourn . . .*
> *Blessed are the meek . . .*
> *Blessed are those who hunger and thirst for righteousness . . .*
> *Blessed are the merciful . . .*
> *Blessed are the pure in heart . . .*
> *Blessed are the peacemakers . . .*
> *Blessed are those who are persecuted for righteousness' sake . . .*
> *Love your enemies and pray for those who persecute you.*
> (Matthew 5:1-10, 44 NRSV)

Based on the world's ideas of wisdom and power, that's just foolishness. Those are not the folks who get blessed in this world. Those are the folks who end up on the short end of the stick or, worse, get nailed to one. The cross looks like weakness to those who think that we can save ourselves and change our world through sheer human determination or economic, political, and military power.

A Disciple's Heart: Daily Workbook

But to those who know their own weakness—to those who know that they are powerless to save themselves or to change the world—the cross becomes the sign of the undeserved, unearned forgiveness and grace of God that has the power to change and transform their lives.

As a follower of Christ whose life was rooted in Scripture, Martin Luther King, Jr., used the term *maladjusted* to describe the extreme love of Christ. He said that while everyone wants to live a well-adjusted life, there are some things in our social order to which he was proud to be maladjusted—things such as segregation, discrimination, religious bigotry, unfair economic conditions, militarism, and violence. He called upon all of us to be maladjusted, saying that the world's salvation might reside with those who are maladjusted.[16]

Every now and then we catch a glimpse of this kind of love in a particular person's life, and when we do the world takes notice. A contemporary example would be the world's fascination with Pope Francis. An obsession to be more like Christ is the driving force in the life of *every* disciple. It is the foolishness and weakness that ends up being the wisdom and power of God.

Your Reflections

- When/how have you found the words of Matthew 5:1-10 to be true in your life? *I witnessed the civil rights march on Washington & heard Martin Luther King speak in DC and it changed rights for blacks*

- In your own words, how would you explain the "foolishness of the cross"? *It seems foolish to love those who hate you, but many lives have been changed by love*

- How has this "foolishness" changed and transformed your life? *I have refused to let hate drive my life & have been blessed many times*

- In what ways is the extremism of love evident in your life?

The love I have received from many people & the love I have shared through Habitat

Your Guide to Prayer and Action

God, I pray for the awareness of your presence within me—in my brokenness and in my strength. I pray for the knowledge of your will and the power to carry it out. May I live the foolishness of the cross and of the Beatitudes today and every day. Help me to surrender, to be meek, and to be merciful and forgiving. I know that I cannot do this in my own will or power but only because you are in me. Only your presence and power, made real in perfect weakness—can do it. Amen.

- Follow the instructions on page 120 for a time of centering prayer. Read aloud 1 Corinthians 1:18-2:2 to begin your prayer period, or use another passage of your own choosing.
- Read through Matthew 5:1-12 and pray the Beatitudes.
- Go to an online Bible dictionary and research the meanings of key words used in the Beatitudes.

WEEK 6
ALL THE WAY TO HEAVEN

While mountain climbing in the Swiss Alps in the summer of 1941, twenty-year-old Robert Matthias Barth tragically fell to his death. Four days later, his father, renowned theologian Karl Barth, preached in the memorial service. A theological giant became a broken-hearted parent whose grief was framed by a faith that was big enough to encompass the pain of every parent who has ever lost a child.

Barth focused the congregation's attention on the words *now* and *then* in 1 Corinthians 13:12-13: "For *now* we see in a mirror, dimly, but *then* we will see face to face. *Now* I know only in part; *then* I will know fully, even as I have been fully known. And *now* faith, hope, and love abide, these three; and the greatest of these is love" (NRSV, emphasis added). He told those gathered that both the Now and the Then are "deeply and indissolubly united." Then, speaking of his son's death, he said this: "We stand with [Christ] at the border where the Now and the Then touch each other."[1]

The border between Now and Then is where we live out the journey toward Christian perfection. In the Now, we acknowledge that we are not yet the persons we will be. Then is when God's saving work of grace has been completed in our lives and our world. We live in the reality that God's reign is present with us now to the full degree that we live within it. At the same time, we look with confidence to the way that rule will be completed when God's saving purpose is fulfilled in this creation.

Based on Paul's words in 1 Corinthians 13, Barth named the three essential qualities that link our Now with God's Then: faith, hope, and love. Our discipleship is always a response of faith in the love and grace of God. It is not something we earn or deserve but is solely a gift we receive through faith. It is a gift that begins Now in the assurance that it will be completed Then. Our hope for perfection is based on the assurance that "the one who started a good work in you will stay with you to complete the job by the day of Christ Jesus" (Philippians 1:6).

This week we will explore the geography of the boundary between Now and Then in the assurance that both the imperfections of our Now and the perfect fulfillment of God's Then are bound together in the love of God in Christ.

99

WEEK 6: DAY 1
A LONG OBEDIENCE

Scripture Reading

Read Hebrews 6:1, 11:8-10.

Today's Message

The Green Cathedral was an outdoor worship center at a Methodist youth camp called Wesley Woods, where I learned to say yes to the call of discipleship. Those early experiences set the direction that I have been imperfectly following ever since.

Years later I found a way to describe that journey using the words of the German philosopher Friedrich Nietzsche. Though Nietzsche was wrong on many levels, he was right about this:

> The essential thing "in heaven and in earth" is . . . that there should be long OBEDIENCE in the same direction, there thereby results, and has always resulted in the long run, something which has made life worth living.[2]

It's true for every athlete who competes in the Olympics. It's true for every musician, artist, or scholar. It's true for everyone who attempts to raise a healthy family or build a successful business. And it's true for every disciple of Jesus Christ who strives to live the Christian life. The essential thing is a long obedience in the same direction.

Hebrews 6:1 offers the soul-stirring challenge, "Let us go on toward perfection" (NRSV). The biblical model for this journey is Abraham, who was constantly "looking forward to a city that has foundations, whose architect and builder is God" (Hebrews 11:10).

That is what it means to be a follower of Jesus Christ whose life is continually centering in loving God and loving others. What makes the difference is a long, persistent, sometimes stumbling, always imperfect obedience to the words, way, and will of Jesus Christ. It's an obedience that acknowledges our imperfect lives Now while constantly moving toward the perfection of life Then.

Sure enough, there are decisive moments along the way when we choose to follow Christ down some new path; formative moments when we choose to take the next step in our discipleship. But over the long haul, the essential thing is a long obedience in the same direction.

The journey that began for Benjamin Ingham in the Holy Club at Oxford set the direction for the long obedience of his life. After graduation, he went with John and Charles Wesley as missionaries to Georgia. He later returned to his home in Yorkshire where he began gatherings for Bible study, hymn singing, and prayer in his mother's house. Following the pattern he had established in Oxford, he also spent a significant part of his time teaching poor children to read.

A Disciple's Heart: Daily Workbook

One of my great joys in ministry has been my relationship with aging saints whose lifelong faithfulness has demonstrated the long obedience of discipleship. They prove Nietzsche to be correct when he said that discipleship is what makes life worth living. And yet, each disciple has a choice to make—will we continue this long obedience?

Paul's relationship with Demas illustrates this choice. In his letter to the Colossians, Paul listed Demas as one of his companions (Colossians 4:14) but later he told Timothy, "Demas has fallen in love with the present world and has deserted me" (2 Timothy 4:10).

> "By Methodists I mean, a people who profess to pursue (in whatsoever measure they have attained) holiness of heart and life . . . in justice, mercy, and truth, or universal love filling the heart, and governing the life."[3]
> —John Wesley

Any Olympic athlete could decide somewhere along the way that the demands are just too difficult, the work too hard, and the effort too intense. He or she could end up watching the Olympics from a recliner rather than competing for the gold medal.

In the same way, we always have the choice of stopping somewhere along the journey of discipleship. We could decide that this is as far as we are willing to go toward being perfected in love. Or, by the grace of God and the power of the Holy Spirit, we can keep reaching out to what lies ahead and continue following Christ in a long obedience in the same direction.

Nietzsche said that the long obedience is what makes life worth living. Wherever you are along the pathway of discipleship, the question is for you. Will you settle down somewhere along the way? Or will you continue growing as a disciple whose life is centering in loving God and loving others?

Your Reflections

- Think of something to which you have been obedient when times were difficult. What kept you going?

  Prayer has always help me through difficult times

- Have there been times in your Christian journey when you settled down and stopped growing? If so, what got you going again?

  Yes as my career & family life obligation my Christian life didnt grow. As I reached retirement I focused more on my spiritual life.

- Remember and name a decisive moment when you chose to follow Christ down a new path in a new direction.

  When I joined Alexandria First Christian Church

- Is Christ calling you to a new path now? What do you think lies ahead?

  I need to be a better witness to my family & friends

Your Guide to Prayer and Action

Lord, instill in me a heart that is obedient to you and to the call to love. May I engage the spiritual practices that will form me with peaceful obedience now and all of my days. When I fall, lift me up. When I rise, remind me that it is by the mercy of God. Empower me to move forward to what lies ahead. Amen.

- Pray through Hebrews 6:1, 11:8-10 using *Lectio Divina* (refer to the steps on page 119). Whatever word or phrase God gives you from the Scripture during this time, use it throughout the day to center your thoughts.
- Reread Hebrews 11:8-10. Pray and journal about where you are going as well as the inheritance that you receive now and the eternal inheritance that awaits you in the future.

Week 6: Day 2
Holy Partners in a Heavenly Calling

Scripture Readings

Read Revelation 7:9-17 and Hebrews 3:1.

Today's Message

Daniel Burnham was the visionary architect whose imagination gave birth to the Chicago World's Fair in 1893. John Root, his partner in the project, was also an accomplished musician. The fair was barely lines on paper when Root died with pneumonia. The relative who was with Root at the time told Burnham that in the final moments Root ran his fingers along the side of his bed as if he were playing the piano. "'Do you hear that?' he whispered. 'Isn't that wonderful? That's what I call music.'"[4]

When the Apostle John imagined life in heaven, he could hear the music. We know this because the Book of Revelation is structured around his images of the heavenly throngs around the throne, singing praise to God. I imagine John laying down his pen and saying, "Now, that's what I call music!"

William Willimon picked up on that imagery when he described life on this side of the resurrection as "a long choir rehearsal" for heaven:

> One day, there before the throne, we shall take our places among the myriads of myriads, with the humpback whales and bullfinches, the wolves and the lemurs, with those whom we have loved (and presumably, with the myriads whom we have despised), all singing with one voice, "Blessing and honor and glory and might to the Lamb."[5]

You don't have to be able to carry a tune in a bucket to appreciate the metaphor. Life on this side of death is a choir rehearsal for heaven. The way we live, think, and act now is the way we tune our souls to the music of God's redemptive purpose that will ultimately be fulfilled through the risen Christ. It's the way we get our feet moving to the rhythm of the life to come. It's the way we join our voices in the song of salvation. Now, that's what I call music!

In one of today's Scriptures the writer of the letter to the Hebrews names us when he names the first readers as "holy partners in a heavenly calling" (3:1 NRSV). It's another way of affirming God's call to "holiness of heart and life." We are holy or "set apart" because . . .

- we share a special relationship with God.
- we have invited God to work in and through us.
- we refuse to allow our lives to be determined by the lowest common denominator of the moral, social, political, or economic assumptions of the world in which we live.
- we shape our thoughts and actions around the values of the kingdom of God revealed in Jesus Christ.
- we live and serve not as isolated individuals but as partners with our brothers and sisters in the body of Christ.
- we march to a different drummer, sing a different tune, move to a different rhythm because we have heard a hint of the music of heaven, the fulfillment of God's redemptive purpose in Christ.

> "The church is the community that lives ahead of time, the people who say now what may one day be said of all, once God gets what God wants—'Your kingdom come. Your will be done, on earth as it is in heaven.' "[6]
> —William W. Willimon

Somewhere along the way I heard a professor say that the purpose of our talk about heaven is not to impart knowledge but to provide orientation. The biblical visions of heaven are not given so that we can determine how many karats are in the golden streets or obtain the exact measurements of the Holy City. They are not given to provide a prophetic calendar for the events of the twenty-first century in which our nation always manages to come out on God's side. They are the imaginative images by which we set the direction for our lives. The goal of the holy life is not to escape this earth but to play our part in God's redemption of it. Our sense of what life is like beyond death determines the way we live right now.

People who see themselves as "holy partners in a heavenly calling" are never satisfied with this world as it is, with all its violence, bigotry, racism, poverty, pain, suffering, and death. Rather, they are always investing themselves in the way they believe God intends for this world to become. They see all of life as a choir rehearsal for heaven.

Architect and city planner Daniel Burnham is often quoted as saying, "Make no little plans; they have no magic to stir men's blood and probably themselves will not be realized. Make big plans; aim high in hope and work."[7] There's nothing higher in hope and work than the heavenly calling that is ours in the risen Christ.

I have no idea what kind of music they sing in heaven. My guess is that on any given day you can hear everything from Beethoven to Bono. But I do know the way the early American Methodists sang about it. It's a song of aspiration that sets the direction for our lives:

> On Jordan's stormy banks I stand,
> And cast a wishful eye
> To Canaan's fair and happy land,
> Where my possessions lie.

The refrain is both an affirmation and an invitation.

> I am bound for the promised land,
> I am bound for the promised land;
> Oh, who will come and go with me?
> I am bound for the promised land.[8]

Do you hear that? Isn't that wonderful? Now, that's what I call music!

Your Reflections

- What kind of music most deeply connects you to the divine?

  Classical music & hymns

- What is your image of heaven? How does your idea of heaven influence the way you live today?

  A place where people enjoy life together

- In what ways do you see yourself as a holy partner in a holy calling?

  I try to serve others in need

- Search the Internet for a site where you can hear "On Jordan's Stormy Banks I Stand." What difference does it make for you to know that you are bound for the Promised Land and to know that others are making that journey with you?

Your Guide to Prayer and Action

God, I believe that I am bound for the Promised Land! Thank you for empowering me and my faith community to do your work now as we rehearse for heaven. Today may I experience the rhythm of your love and your heavenly calling as I live in hope! Amen.

- Practice the Saint Ignatius prayer method following the instructions on page 121. Use Revelation 7:9-17, one of the narrative Scriptures listed on page 121, or a narrative passage of your own choosing.
- Ask other friends or members of your small group to share their favorite visual image of heaven. How does sharing these different images make you feel about life beyond death?

A Disciple's Heart: Daily Workbook

WEEK 6: DAY 3
RELENTLESS IN DOING GOOD

Scripture Reading

Read Galatians 6:4-10.

Today's Message

> Walk together children.
> Don't you get weary.
> There's a great camp meeting in the Promised Land.[9]

The truth is that any of us can get weary along the pathway of discipleship, particularly when we confront the seemingly intractable evils that go against the grain of our journey toward Christian perfection in ourselves and in our world.

That's why the Apostle Paul told the Thessalonians, "Be not weary in well doing" (2 Thessalonians 3:13 KJV). He repeated that instruction to the Galatians when he wrote, "Let us not be weary in well doing: for in due season we shall reap, if we faint not" (Galatians 6: 9 KJV).

John Wesley echoed Paul in the last letter he wrote before his death. He was writing to William Wilberforce, the British abolitionist who had come to faith in Christ through the influence of the Methodist revival and who spent his career opposing slavery. It would be difficult to miss the passion in Wesley's encouragement for Wilberforce to continue his opposition to what Wesley called "that execrable villainy which is the scandal of religion."[10]

> Unless God has raised you up for this very thing, you will be worn out by the opposition . . . But if God be for you, who can be against you? Are all of them together stronger than God? O be not weary of well doing! Go on, in the name of God and in the power of his might, till even American slavery (the vilest that ever saw the sun) shall vanish away before it.[11]

Wesley was equally relentless in challenging other institutional injustices of his day, particularly economic inequity that resulted in poverty, starvation, slavery, and war. He called the early Methodists to an inner transformation of the heart that expressed itself in both personal and systemic change. He saw the way the economic, political, and social structures of his time were participants in the problem and could become part of the solution. For example, in confronting widespread starvation among the lower classes, he called for grain to be used in the production of bread rather than being distilled for gin. According to Paul Chilcote, though Wesley was not a pacifist, he saw war as the "sum of all sin."[12]

> Who now against each other rise,
> The nations of the earth, constrain
> To follow after peace, and prize
> The blessings of thy righteous reign,
> The joys of unity to prove,
> The paradise of perfect love![13]
> —Charles Wesley

The issues we confront today are consistent with the issues that the Wesleys confronted:

- Economic injustice continues, resulting in an epidemic of obesity in one part of the world and massive starvation in others.
- Although slavery was abolished in Great Britian and America, racial prejudice continues to pollute our culture—and in some parts of the world results in ethnic conflict.
- The nations and the peoples of the world continue to take up arms against each other in the madness of war.
- The contagion of violence infects our nation with an irrational addiction to guns.

Add to these concerns the crisis of environmental destruction and global warming, and we have more than enough reasons to take Paul's warning seriously:

> *Those who plant only for their own benefit will harvest devastation from their selfishness, but those who plant for the benefit of the Spirit will harvest eternal life from the Spirit. Let's not get tired of doing good, because in time we'll have a harvest if we don't give up. (Galatians 6:8-9)*

Christian perfection is not only about the transformation of the individual heart. It also is about the way people with transformed hearts participate in God's transformation of the world. The Spirit that gave Wesley a "strangely warmed" heart is the same Spirit that planted within the Methodist tradition a fiery passion for human rights, social justice, and peace.

John Wesley did not live long enough to see the end of the slave trade in England, but it was enough for him to know that he had done what he could to help make it happen. In the same way, we may not see our visions for social change accomplished, but may it be enough for us to know that we have played our part in God's transformation of the world.

Your Reflections

- Paul tells us to "be not weary." Reflect on a time that you were weary because of the good you were doing. What about it wore you out?

Sometimes I tire of approving glasses for the needy. The fact that some people are working the system.

A Disciple's Heart: Daily Workbook

- Environmental destruction, violence, war, child abuse, hunger, human trafficking, discrimination, inequality, and poverty are just some of the evils that we encounter in the world today. Write about the issue that most infuriates you or breaks your heart and why. *The greed that drives some to oppose taxes that will be used to help bring about education & support that will lift up the poor in our country and around the world*

- If you were to write a letter of encouragement to someone who is working to bring about change in the world today, to whom would you write and why? Take time to write that letter. *Tim Kaine*

- What cause is so important to you that you would be willing to invest yourself in it even if you do not see the goal accomplished in your lifetime? *Better housing for those in need*

Your Guide to Prayer and Action

God, sometimes I am weary, and other times I am consumed by the things of this world at the expense of doing good to counter the crises of the world. Plant and nurture in me a strangely warmed heart that emerges in a fiery passion for injustices that grieve your heart. Amen.

- Pray through Galatians 6:4-10 using *Lectio Divina* (refer to the steps on page 119). Whatever word or phrase God gives you from the Scripture during this time, use it throughout the day to center your thoughts.
- What can you do to address the issue that most infuriates you or breaks your heart, which you named above?

WEEK 6: DAY 4
A LIFETIME OF GLAD REUNIONS

Scripture Reading
Read Revelation 21:1-7.

Today's Message
Earlier this week we shared our favorite images of heaven. I grew up singing "I've Got a Mansion Just Over the Hilltop" and picturing a big house on a hill. It turns out that it looked a lot like Downton Abbey.

As I have matured in my faith, my images of heaven have grown too. Today I would define heaven with imaginative pictures to describe the fulfillment of God's saving work in us and in this creation. Heaven is the completion of everything that God revealed in the life, death, and resurrection of Jesus Christ. In Karl Barth's terms, heaven is where Now becomes Then. It's the fulfillment of that prayer that God's kingdom will come and God's will be done on earth as it is in heaven.

There's a lot I don't know about heaven, but there are a few things of which I am pretty sure. One is that in heaven we will know and be known more completely than we have ever been known before. Paul told the Corinthians, "Now we see a reflection in a mirror; then we will see face-to-face. Now I know partially, but then I will know completely in the same way that I have been completely known" (1 Corinthians 13:12).

My uncle Frank was, in many ways, the glue that held our extended family together. In his funeral service, my brother-preacher shared words he had inherited from one of his pastoral mentors. He said that after years of offering biblically sound, intellectually responsible, and totally unsatisfactory answers to people's questions about heaven, he decided to be like Jesus and answer their question with another question. When people asked, "Will I see my loved ones in heaven?" he replied, "Would it be heaven if you don't?"

My brother went on to explain what the pastor who had mentored him had said, which was that the longer he was in the ministry, the less interested he was in trying to provide intellectual explanations for life beyond death. He said that if by eternal life we mean the possibility of what he called "glad reunion," then we're talking about something that is absolutely priceless and absolutely worth hoping for.

That word *reunion* hooked my attention. Whatever else it may be, I believe that heaven will be an infinite lifetime of glad reunions. That's not to say that there won't be surprises. God's grace may be a lot larger than our expectations. We'd better be prepared to run into some unexpected "relatives" at the reunion table. But even with them, by God's grace it will become a glad reunion.

I also believe that heaven is not off on a distant cloud but right here, close at hand. Celtic spirituality talks about "thin spaces." They are places where the distance between heaven and earth collapses and we experience the divine. It's what we affirm in the Apostles' Creed when we say that we believe in "the communion of saints." In other words, the people we have loved and who have shown us what it looks like to be a follower of Jesus are not that far away. In a sense, they are right here, present with us, to inspire, challenge, and hold us accountable for our discipleship.

> "I am a creature of a day, passing through life as an arrow through the air.... I want to know one thing,—the way to heaven; how to land safe on that happy shore. God himself has condescended to teach the way: For this very end he came from heaven."[14]
> —John Wesley

John Wesley called All Saints' Day "a festival I dearly love."[15] The longer I've been in ministry, the more I've come to love it too. Each year we light a candle as we call the names of those church members who have died in the past year. Without fail, I speak names of people who have loved me, supported me, and challenged me to be my best. Their continuing presence in my life is more than just a memory. It's as if they are right here, close at hand, in the "thin space" where earth and heaven meet.

Several weeks ago you named some of the people who have influenced your life as a follower of Christ. While some of those may still be present with us, others may have gone on into life after death. Whether they are here on earth or have taken up residence in heaven, their presence in the communion of saints is still available to encourage and challenge you. By faith, you can look forward to an infinite lifetime of glad reunions.

Your Reflections

- What difference does it make for you to believe that in heaven we will know and be known more completely than we have been known on earth?

  It means that we should try very hard to live a good life and serve others and reach out to them in love

- Search online or find in a hymnal the text for Charles Wesley's hymn "Come, Let Us Join our Friends Above." Which verse of the hymn speaks most deeply to you?

- Who are the people you most hope to be reunited with in heaven? Why?

My parents and many grandparents

- Describe a "thin space"—a time when you have experienced the connection between the earthly and the divine. If nothing comes to mind, describe what you imagine it might be like.

Your Guide to Prayer and Action

Thank you, God, for the saints who have gone before me—those who have loved me at my best and worst—and for the encouragement and support I have received that has shaped me into the person I am now and the person I will become. May I always live with the hope of the new life to come. Amen.

- Practice the Saint Ignatius prayer method following the instructions on page 121. Use Revelation 21:1-7, one of the narrative Scriptures listed on page 121, or a narrative passage of your own choosing.
- Write below your reflections on our belief in the "communion of saints." What does that particular affirmation mean for you?

A Disciple's Heart: Daily Workbook

WEEK 6: DAY 5
ANTICIPATE YOUR HEAVEN

Scripture Reading
Read Revelation 1:1-8.

Today's Message
I was preparing for the memorial service of one of the saints of our congregation when some unfamiliar lines jumped out at me in Charles Wesley's hymn "O, For a Thousand Tongues to Sing":

> In Christ, your head, you then shall know,
> Shall feel your sins forgiven;
> Anticipate your heaven below,
> And own that love is heaven.[16]

To *anticipate* is to feel or realize something before it happens. "Anticipate your heaven" means living Now the way we believe the world will be Then. It means shaping our lives in this world in ways that are consistent with the way the world will be when God's kingdom comes and God's will is done on earth as it is in heaven.

In other words, heaven is the fulfillment of everything we are already becoming. Heaven is what the New Testament writers mean when they use the Greek word *telios*. It's the end toward which all things are moving. Heaven is the consummation of God's work of salvation for the whole creation; the final fulfillment of our growth toward perfection. Anticipating heaven means that . . .

> Let us for this faith contend,
> Sure salvation is the end;
> Heaven already is begun,
> Everlasting life is won.[17]
> —Charles Wesley

- we care about this earth Now because Then the renewed creation will be the place where God will be at home with God's people (Revelation 21:3).
- we work for peace Now because we know that Then swords will be turned into plowshares and spears into pruning hooks and people will not learn war anymore (Isaiah 2:4 NRSV).
- we work to heal racial and ethnic division Now because we know that Then heaven will be filled with people from every race, tongue, and nation (Revelation 7:8-9).
- we invite others to become disciples of Christ Now because we know that Then every knee will bow and every tongue confess that Jesus Christ is Lord (Philippians 2:10-11 NRSV).
- we care for one another in Christian love Now because we know that Then God will wipe away every tear from our eyes (Revelation 21:4).

- we feed the hungry, heal the sick, clothe the naked, visit the prisoners, and seek economic justice for the poor Now because Jesus said that this is the way that every nation will be judged Then (Matthew 25:31-46).

In John's Gospel, the phrase "eternal life" does not refer to an other-worldly, pie-in-the-sky-by-and-by existence after death. Eternal life is a quality of living in relationship with God that begins as a finite reality Now and that will be infinitely fulfilled Then.

Through my years in ministry, I've observed that people generally die the way they live. If a person has lived a self-enclosed life, shut off from other people, grumpy and mean, that's probably the way he or she will die. But if a person has lived life openly, sharing the good gifts of love, faith, and joy, that's probably the way he or she will die.

If people die the way they lived, the corollary is that we need to live the way we hope to die. Heaven begins in the way we live right here and now.

My sister-in-law's mother, Marge, died the week after Easter at age ninety-three. She was incorrigibly optimistic. Everything she saw, every person she met, everything she experienced was wonderful and worthy of celebration.

On Easter Sunday, someone snapped a picture of her surrounded by her great-grandchildren. Because of the dementia, she could not have told you their names, but the picture captures the smile and laughter that was always a part of her life. The day after Easter, she had a major hemorrhage in her brain. Gazing out of the ambulance window, she kept saying, "Wow! Wow! Wonderful!"

There was, of course, no way of knowing what she was thinking. But perhaps, like the Apostle John, she was catching a glimpse of heaven. In any case, she died the way she had lived, saying, "Wow! Wonderful!"

In calling us to "own that love is heaven," Charles Wesley's hymn takes us back to the heart of the matter, which is always a matter of the heart. The heaven toward which the journey of Christian perfection is taking us is nothing less than the completion of God's work of love in us and in the whole creation.

We began this study with Charles Wesley's words: "Changed from glory into glory / Till in heaven we take our place." C.S. Lewis expressed the same hope when he said that Jesus' command to be perfect (Matthew 5:48 NRSV) is not "idealistic gas" or a "command to do the impossible." Instead, Lewis said,

> If we let Him—for we can prevent Him, if we choose—He will make the feeblest and filthiest of us into . . . a dazzling, radiant, immortal creature, pulsating all through with such energy and joy and wisdom and love as we cannot now imagine. . . . The process will be long and in parts very painful; but that is what we are in for. Nothing less. He meant what He said.[18]

As we come to the end of this study, our hope is that the journey toward perfection that the Spirit has begun in your life will be an end without an ending, an ongoing journey that will continue God's work of love in your heart all the way to heaven.

Your Reflections

- What does the term *eternal life* mean to you? What difference does the definition given here—a quality of living in relationship with God—make for you?

  Peace
  It means happiness & love

- How are you anticipating heaven in the Now?

  I am trying to live a useful and faithful life with love for others

- Which of the seven actions indicated by bullets above in Today's Message is most challenging for you?

  Inviting others to church

- How have you observed that people die the way they live? What difference does that observation make for you?

  There was a difference in how my mother and my mother-in-law lived and died

Your Guide to Prayer and Action

Father, Son, and Holy Spirit, I pray that I might anticipate heaven Now as I await your completion of love in me and in the whole creation Then. Until then, may I love my family, friends, and enemies in the way of Jesus of Nazareth. Amen.

- Practice the Saint Ignatius prayer method following the instructions on page 121. Use Revelation 1:1-8, one of the narrative Scriptures listed on page 121, or a narrative passage of your own choosing.
- What new discoveries have you made during this study? What specific changes will you make because of those discoveries? Write them below.

- Share with a friend or with your small group the next steps you intend to take on your journey toward Christian perfection.

TWENTY-TWO HOLY CLUB QUESTIONS

1. Am I consciously or unconsciously creating the impression that I am better than I really am? In other words, am I a hypocrite?

2. Am I honest in all my acts and words, or do I exaggerate?

3. Do I confidentially pass on to others what has been said to me in confidence?

4. Can I be trusted?

5. Am I a slave to dress, friends, work, or habits?

6. Am I self-conscious, self-pitying, or self-justifying?

7. Did the Bible live in me today?

8. Do I give the Bible time to speak to me every day?

9. Am I enjoying prayer?

10. When did I last speak to someone else of my faith?

11. Do I pray about the money I spend?

12. Do I get to bed on time and get up on time?

13. Do I disobey God in anything?

14. Do I insist upon doing something about which my conscience is uneasy?

15. Am I defeated in any part of my life?

16. Am I jealous, impure, critical, irritable, touchy, or distrustful?

17. How do I spend my spare time?

18. Am I proud?

19. Do I thank God that I am not as other people, especially as the Pharisees who despised the publican?

20. Is there anyone whom I fear, dislike, disown, criticize, hold a resentment toward or disregard? If so, what am I doing about it?

21. Do I grumble or complain constantly?

22. Is Christ real to me?

From http://hopefaithprayer.com/john-wesley-holy-club-questions/.

A Disciple's Heart: Daily Workbook

LECTIO DIVINA

About *Lectio Divina*

Lectio Divina (pronounced lektīō dĭvīnə), which means "Divine Reading," is an ancient practice of contemplative Bible study that allows the Bible to read you rather than you reading the Bible. There are generally four movements or steps in *Lectio Divina*:

1. *Lectio*: A slow, meditative reading of Scripture.

2. *Meditatio*: Thinking or reflecting on the word or phrase. (Why did it stand out? Why did it strike your heart?)

3. *Oratio*: Responding to the word or phrase. Tell God how you feel and what you think.

4. *Contemplatio*: Resting in God in silence—without words, thoughts, or images.

Adapted from M. Basil Pennington, *Lectio Divina: Renewing the Ancient Practice of Praying the Scriptures* (New York: Crossroad, 1998), 132–133.

Instructions for a Time of Lectio Divina

Say a silent prayer, believing that God is going to speak to you.

1. (*Lectio*) Select a short passage of Scripture, ideally no more than one to five verses. A great place to start is the Psalms or Gospels, or choose one of the Scripture Readings from the week.
   - Read it aloud very, very slowly. Scripture is meant to be heard with the ears and soul. This reading will give you the context of the passage.
   - Prayerfully read the passage a second and third time. Let the Scripture read you, rather than you reading the Scripture. As you are listening intently, wait until a word or phrase from the Scripture touches your heart. Then stop!

2. (*Meditatio*) Say the word or phrase to yourself and begin to reflect on it.
   - Think about why that word or phrase struck you. Ask yourself, Why did it strike my heart? How is it pertinent to my life?

3. (*Oratio*) Respond to the word or phrase from your heart.
   - Tell God your feelings either by writing in a journal or talking silently to God.

4. (*Contemplatio*) Rest in God in silence.
   - As your mind begins to wander, use the word or phrase God gave you to center yourself again.

CENTERING PRAYER

About Centering Prayer

The purpose of centering prayer is not to create peace or empty your mind but to cultivate relationship with Christ through silence. It goes beyond thoughts and visual images to the core or center of your being. The focus of centering prayer is the desire to be with God, who is within you, to allow God to work within you, and to silently surrender to God's love.

Basil Pennington's Method of Centering Prayer*

Sit relaxed and be quiet.

1. Be in faith and love to God who dwells in the center of your being.

2. Take up a love word and let it be gently present, supporting your being to God in faith-filled love.

3. Whenever you become aware of anything, simply, gently return to the Lord with the use of your prayer word.

Another way to describe this method:

1. Be with God within.

2. Use a word to stay.

3. Use the word to return.

*Adapted from M. Basil Pennington's *Centering Prayer: Renewing an Ancient Christian Prayer Form* (New York: Doubleday, 2001), xv–xvi.

Instructions for a Time of Centering Prayer

1. Select your centering word. It can be any word to focus on as you pray (e.g., *light, love, Jesus, mercy, peace, Abba, Maranatha, Yahweh*). You will keep this word throughout the prayer period. If your mind wanders, return gently to your centering word.

2. Assume the proper position. Sit with your back straight in a chair, feet on the floor, and your hands positioned comfortably on your legs. Make sure you are in a location that is quiet and as distraction free as possible.

3. Read a short passage of Scripture—perhaps one of the Scripture Readings from the week. Then lightly shut your eyes and begin the prayer period. Generally, centering prayer is done for twenty minutes. If you want to start with a lesser amount of time, try ten or fifteen minutes.

4. Say your centering word silently for the allotted time.

5. Conclude by praying the Lord's Prayer aloud.

SAINT IGNATIUS PRAYER METHOD

About Saint Ignatius Prayer Method

Ignatius of Loyola was the founder of the Society of Jesus (Jesuits) and is said to be the originator of a form of prayer that engages the Scriptures imaginatively. Saint Ignatius believed that praying in this way shaped one's life. It is ideal to use a Scripture passage that is narrative in nature; in other words, the characters are living out a story of faith.

Guidelines for Using the Saint Ignatius Prayer Method*

- Place yourself into the scene as one of the characters so as to experience it more fully in mind, body, and spirit.
- Enter the story as a careful observer—a fly on the wall.
- Ignatius commended the use of the senses in this type of meditation. You attempt to taste, hear, smell, and feel the passage.
- You may become one of the characters, experiencing it from his or her point of view. Most of all, the hope is to help you perceive the narrative from the viewpoint of Jesus.

*Based on material from Dawson et al., *Companions in Christ Participant Book* (Nashville: Upper Room Books, 2001), 96–98.

Instructions for a Time of Saint Ignatius Prayer Method

Begin with a brief prayer.

1. Choose a Scripture passage that is narrative in nature. In other words, the characters are living out a story of faith. Many of the stories Jesus told are conducive to this prayer method (Matthew 9:2-8 or Mark 2:1-12; Mark 8:1-10; Mark 9:2-13; Luke 2:1-14; Luke 10:38-42; John 2:1-12).

2. Read through the passage to gain an understanding of the characters, surroundings, and overall context. Reflect on what you read during a time of silence.

3. Read the passage a second time, allowing your imagination to bring you into the story. As you read, visualize the sights, smell the smells, hear the sounds, taste the tastes, and feel the surroundings. Reflect on the experience during a time of silence.

4. Read the passage a third and final time, using your imagination to enter the story as one of the characters. Allow yourself to experience the emotions, beliefs, or thoughts of a person in the narrative. Reflect on the experience during a time of silence.

5. After the final time of reflection and silence, say the Lord's Prayer aloud.

NOTES

Introduction

1. *Journal of John Wesley,* http://www.ccel.org/ccel/wesley/journal.vi.ii.xvi.html.

2. *The Book of Common Prayer,* "Administration of the Holy Communion," http://justus.anglican.org/resources/bcp/1789Selections/Communion.htm.

3. "O for a Heart to Praise My God," Charles Wesley, 1742, *The United Methodist Hymnal* (Nashville: The United Methodist Publishing House, 1989), 417.

4. "Letter to Robert C. Brackenbury, Esq.," *The Works of John Wesley,* ed.Thomas Jackson, 14 vols., 3rd ed. (London: Wesleyan Methodist Book Room, 1872; reprint ed.: Grand Rapids: Zondervan, 1958–1959), XIII Letters: 9.

5. Richard P. Heitzenrater, ed., *Diary of an Oxford Methodist: Benjamin Ingham, 1733–1734* (Durham, NC: Duke University Press, 1985), 16.

6. "Love Divine, All Loves Excelling," Charles Wesley, 1747, *The United Methodist Hymnal,* 384.

Week 1

1. *A Disciple's Path,* James Harnish with Justin LaRosa (Nashville: Abingdon Press, 2012), 16.

2. "O for a Heart to Praise My God," Charles Wesley, 1742, *The United Methodist Hymnal,* 417.

3. "I Sought the Lord," Words: Anonymous, 1890, *The United Methodist Hymnal,* 341.

4. From *The Book of Discipline of The United Methodist Church*—2012 . Copyright © 2012 by The United Methodist Publishing House; ¶330, p. 250. Used by permission.

5. "Telios," http://biblehub.com/greek/5046.htm

6. Kathleen Norris, *Amazing Grace: A Vocabulary of Faith* (New York: Riverhead Books, 1998), 56.

7. "What Shall I Do, My God to Love?" Charles Wesley, 1742, http://cyberhymnal.org/htm/w/s/wsidmgtl.htm.

8. Paul Wesley Chilcote, *John & Charles Wesley: Selections from Their Writing and Hymns,* (Woodstock, VT: Skylight Paths, 2011), 151.

9. "A Plain Account of Christian Perfection," *The Works of John Wesley,* ed. Thomas Jackson, V: 207; also in "The Circumcision of the Heart," http://www.umcmission.org/Find-Resources/John-Wesley-Sermons/Sermon-17-The-Circumcision-of-the-Heart.

10. "A New Generation Expresses Its Skepticism and Frustration with Christianity," The Barna Group, https://www.barna.org/barna-update/teens-nextgen/94-a-new-generation-expresses-its-skepticism-and-frustration-with-christianity#.UypFWqhdXng.

11. Brian Kolodiejchuk, *Mother Teresa: Come By My Light* (New York: Doubleday, 2007), 38.

12. John Ortberg, *The Life You've Always Wanted* (Grand Rapids: Zondervan, 1997), 47.

13. John Wesley, from "Letter to Mr Jonathan Maskew," quoted in *A Guide to Prayer for All Who Seek God,* Norman Shawchuck and Rueben P. Job (Nashville: Upper Room Books, 2003), 138.

14. Norman Shawchuck and Rueben P. Job, *A Guide to Prayer for All Who Seek God* (Nashville: Upper Room Books, 2003), 81.

15. "Love Divine, All Loves Excelling," Charles Wesley, 1747, *The United Methodist Hymnal,* 384.

16. "Christian Perfection," T*he Works of John Wesley,* ed. Thomas Jackson, VI: 5–6.

17. Wesley Covenant Prayer, from *The United Methodist Hymnal,* 607. Used by permission.

Week 2

1. John Wesley, "Salvation by Faith, http://www.umcmission.org/Find-Resources/John-Wesley-Sermons/Sermon-1-Salvation-by-Faith#sthash.sAZpD0X2.dpuf.

2. William H. Willimon, *Who Will Be Saved?* (Nashville: Abingdon, 2008), 3.

3. *The Anchor Bible Dictionary,* ed. David Noel Freedman vol. 5 (New York: Doubleday, 1992), 907–910.

4. Willimon, *Who Will Be Saved?,* 111.

5. "Harmartia," http://biblehub.com/greek/266.htm.

6. William H. Willimon, *United Methodist Beliefs: A Brief Introduction* (Louisville: Westminster John Knox Press, 2007), 16.

7. Willimon, *Who Will Be Saved?,* 127.

8. Ibid., 28.

9. "Amazing Grace," John Newton, 1779, *The United Methodist Hymnal,* 378.

10. James A. Harnish with Justin LaRosa, *A Disciple's Path: Companion Reader* (Nashville: Abingdon Press, 2012), 20.

11. Kenneth Cain Kinghorn, *The Gospel of Grace,* (Nashville: Abingdon Press, 1992), 13.

12. "And Can It Be That I Should Gain," Charles Wesley, 1739, *The United Methodist Hymnal,* 363.

13. Thomas Merton, *Life and Holiness* (New York: Herder and Herder, 1963), vii.

14. Willimon, *Who Will Be Saved?,* 121.

15. "Texas Gov. Perry baptized in same creek as legendary Sam Houston," Jay Root of The Texas Tribune in The Washington Post, April 29 2014, http://www.washingtonpost.com/politics/texas-gov-perry-baptized-in-same-creek-as-legendary-sam-houston/2014/04/29/f8ef4810-cf28-11e3-b812-0c92213941f4_story.html.

16. "O for a Heart to Praise My God," Charles Wesley, 1742, *The United Methodist Hymnal*, 417.

17. "Thanksgiving Over the Water," The Baptismal Covenant 1, *The United Methodist Hymnal*, 36.

18. "Prayer of Humble Access" in "A Service of Word and Table IV," *The United Methodist Hymnal*, 30.

19. *Journal of Charles Wesley*, April 19, 1747 in Paul W. Chilcote, *Recapturing the Wesleys' Vision* (Downers Grove: InterVarsity Press, 2004), 81.

20 "O the Depth of Love Divine," Charles Wesley, 1745, *The United Methodist Hymnal*, 627.

Week 3

1. Trevor Hudson, *Holy Spirit Here and Now* (Cape Town: Struik Christian Books, 2012), 12–13.

2. "Maker, in Whom We Live," Charles Wesley, 1747, *The United Methodist Hymnal*, 88.

3. "Paraklétos," http://biblehub.com/greek/3875.htm.

4. Hudson, *Holy Spirit Here and Now*, 57.

5. N. T. Wright, *Simply Christian* (New York: HarperOne, 2010), 122.

6. "Dross," Merriam-Webster, http://www.merriam-webster.com/dictionary/dross.

7. "Jesus, Thine All-Victorious Love," Charles Wesley, 1740, *The United Methodist Hymnal*, 422.

8. "Letter to Mr. Walter Churchey," *The Works of John Wesley*, ed. Thomas Jackson, XII Letters: 432.

9. E. Stanley Jones, *Victory Through Surrender* (Nashville: Abingdon Press, 1966), 33.

10. Ibid.

11. Norman Shawchuck and Rueben P. Job, *A Guide to Prayer for All Who Seek God*, 129.

Week 4

1. Stephen Bauman, "Faith Matters: In the Company of Others," January 17, 2014, http://www.christchurchnyc.org/app/webroot/img/gallery/File/Faith%20Matters/1.17.14.pdf.

2. Elton Trueblood, *The Company of the Committed*, 35, web.archive.org/web/20110619084436/http://ccel.us/company.ch2.html.

3. Dietrich Bonhoeffer, *Life Together* (San Francisco: HarperSanFrancisco, 1954), 20.

4. Ibid., 19, 21.

5. "Jesus, United by Thy Grace," Charles Wesley, 1742, *The United Methodist Hymnal*, 561.

6. "The Ultimate Face-to-Face Meeting," Carrie's Blog, http://cferenac.blogspot.com/2010/01/ultimate-face-to-face-meeting.html.

7. http://www.umcmission.org/Find-Resources/John-Wesley-Sermons/Sermon-24-Upon-Our
-Lords-Sermon-on-the-Mount-4#sthash.JXdNj1LD.dpuf.

8. "Blest Be the Dear Uniting Love," Charles Wesley, 1742, *The United Methodist Hymnal,* 566.

9. http://www.episcopalchurch.org/lectionary/aelred-abbot-rievaulx-1167

10. Bernard Mayo, ed., *Jefferson Himself,* (Charlottesville: University Press of Virginia, 1942), 295.

11. "If Death My Friend and Me Divide," Charles Wesley, 1762, *The United Methodist Hymnal,* 656.

Week 5

1. John Wesley, "Thoughts Upon Methodism," http://www.imarc.cc/one_meth/vol-02-no-02.html.

2. "Give Me the Faith Which Can Remove," Charles Wesley, 1749, *The United Methodist Hymnal,* 650.

3. Magrey R. deVega, from a sermon delivered to the 2013 Large Church Initiative of The United Methodist Church, April 22–24, 2013, Tampa, Florida.

4. John Wesley, "On Zeal," http://www.umcmission.org/Find-Resources/John-Wesley-Sermons /Sermon-92-On-Zeal#sthash.aqJZL6w6.dpuf.

5. Peter Storey, *And Are We Yet Alive?* (Cape Town: Methodist Publishing House, 2004), 37.

6. The General Rules of the Methodist Church, http://archives.umc.org/interior.asp?mid=1648.

7. Rueben P. Job, *Three Simple Rules* (Nashville: Abingdon Press, 2007), 10.

8. "Lord, I Want to Be a Christian," African American spiritual, *The United Methodist Hymnal,* 402.

9. Collect for St. Bernard of Clairvaux, http://justus.anglican.org/resources/bio/232.html.

10. Sermon XXII "Upon Our Lord's Sermon On The Mount: Discourse Two," *The Works of John Wesley,* ed. Thomas Jackson, V Sermons: 269.

11. C. S. Lewis, *Mere Christianity* (New York: Macmillan, 1943; New York: Touchstone Book, 1996), 154.

12. *The Anchor Bible Dictionary,* vol. 3, 1128.

13. Paul Wesley Chilcote, *Recapturing the Wesleys' Vision,* (Downers Grove: InterVarsity, 2004), 95.

14. Storey, *And Are We Yet Alive?,* 29.

15. See Scott J. Jones, *United Methodist Doctrine: The Extreme Center* (Nashville: Abingdon Press, 2002), and http://extremecenter.com/.

16. Martin Luther King, Jr., *A Testament of Hope* (New York: HarperOne, 2003), 216.

Week 6

1. Karl Barth, quoted in Michael D. Bus, ed. *The Incomplete One* (Grand Rapids: Eerdmans, 2006), 12–13.

2. Friedrich Nietzsche, *Beyond Good and Evil,* http://www.marxists.org/reference/archive /nietzsche/1886/beyond-good-evil/ch05.htm.

3. John Wesley, quoted in Rueben P. Job, *A Wesleyan Spiritual Reader* (Nashville: Abingdon, 1997), 128.

4. Erik Larson, *The Devil in the White City* (New York: Vintage, 2004), 107.

5. Willimon, *Who Will Be Saved?,* 45.

6. Ibid., 58.

7. "Make No Little Plans: Daniel Burnham and the American City," PBS Special, aired September 2010, http://www.pbs.org/program/make-no-little-plans/.

8. "On Jordan's Stormy Banks I Stand," Samuel Stennett, 1787, *The United Methodist Hymnal* (Nashville: The United Methodist Publishing House, 1989), 724.

9. "Walk Together Children," http://pancocojams.blogspot.com/2013/10/walk-together-children -lyrics-examples.html.

10. John Wesley, "Letter to William Wilberforce," https://gbgm-umc.org/umw/wesley/wilber.stm.

11. Ibid.

12. Chilcote, *John & Charles Wesley: Selections from Their Writings and Hymns,* 246.

13. "Our Earth We Now Lament to See," Charles Wesley, 1758, *The United Methodist Hymnal,* 449.

14. John Wesley, Sermons on Several Occasions, vol. 1, preface, http://biblehub.com/library/wesley /sermons_on_several_occasions/preface.htm.

15. http://wesleyanleadership.com/2010/11/01/all-saints-day-a-festival-i-dearly-love/

16. "O For a Thousand Tongues to Sing," Charles Wesley, 1739, *The United Methodist Hymnal,* 57.

17. "Let Us Plead for Faith Alone," Charles Wesley, 1740, *The United Methodist Hymnal,* 385.

18. C. S. Lewis, *Mere Christianity,* 176.